THE 101
BEST
FISHING TRIPS
IN OREGON

The 101 Best Fishing Trips In Oregon

By

DON HOLM

THE CAXTON PRINTERS, LTD.
CALDWELL, IDAHO 83605
1991

First printing October, 1970
Second printing March, 1976
Third printing September, 1980
Fourth printing January, 1985
Fifth printing August, 1991

International Standard Book Number 0-87004-204-1

Library of Congress Catalog Card Number 79-109542

Printed and bound in the United States of America by
The CAXTON PRINTERS, Ltd.
Caldwell, Idaho   83605
155311

TABLE OF CONTENTS

INTRODUCTION - - - - - - - - - - - - - - 13

Part One
SOUTH COAST

Trip
No.

Page

1	NEW RIVER - - - - - - - - - - - -	19
2	MILLICOMA RIVER SHAD - - - - - - -	20
3	STRIPED BASS COUNTRY - - - - - - -	22
4	LOWER ROGUE - - - - - - - - - - -	23
4	HUNTER CREEK - - - - - - - - - -	25
6	PISTOL RIVER - - - - - - - - - - -	26
7	WINCHUCK RIVER - - - - - - - - - -	27
8	CHETCO RIVER - - - - - - - - - - -	28
9	SIUSLAW BAY - - - - - - - - - - -	30
10	SILTCOOS LAKE - - - - - - - - - -	31
11	LOWER UMPQUA - - - - - - - - - -	33
12	TENMILE LAKES - - - - - - - - - -	35
13	COOS RIVER - - - - - - - - - - - -	36
14	COOS BAY - - - - - - - - - - - -	38
15	COQUILLE RIVER - - - - - - - - - -	39
16	ELK RIVER - - - - - - - - - - - -	40
17	SIXES RIVER - - - - - - - - - - -	41
18	SIUSLAW RIVER - - - - - - - - - -	42
19	VULCAN LAKE - - - - - - - - - - -	43

Part Two
NORTH COAST

20	NEHALEM RIVER - - - - - - - - - -	46
21	NEHALEM BAY - - - - - - - - - - -	48

*Trip
No.*   *Page*
22   TILLAMOOK BAY   - - - - - - - - -   50
23   NESTUCCA RIVER   - - - - - - - - -   52
24   NESTUCCA BAY -   - - - - - - - - -   54
25   DEVILS LAKE   - - - - - - - - - -   55
26   SILETZ RIVER   - - - - - - - - - -   57
27   THE SILETZ JAWS - - - - - - - - -   58
28   YAQUINA BAY   - - - - - - - - - -   61
29   ALSEA RIVER   - - - - - - - - - -   62
30   SALMONBERRY RIVER   - - - - - - -   64

Part Three
COLUMBIA RIVER

31   COLUMBIA ESTUARY   - - - - - - - -   68
32   LOWER COLUMBIA - - - - - - - - -   71
33   "RETIREMENT REACH"   - - - - - -   73
34   BONNEVILLE POOL   - - - - - - - -   75
35   CELILO LAKE   - - - - - - - - - -   77
36   LAKE UMATILLA   - - - - - - - - -   79
37   LAKE WALLULA   - - - - - - - - -   81

Part Four
METROPOLITAN

38   LOWER WILLAMETTE   - - - - - - - -   85
39   SAUVIE ISLAND - - - - - - - - - -   87
40   TIMOTHY LAKE   - - - - - - - - - -   88
41   CLACKAMAS RIVER   - - - - - - - -   90
42   MOLALLA RIVER - - - - - - - - - -   92
43   PUDDING RIVER - - - - - - - - - -   93

Part Five
WILLAMETTE WATERSHED

44   MAINSTEM WILLAMETTE - - - - - - -   97
45   WALDO LAKE   - - - - - - - - - -   99
46   THE SANTIAMS -   - - - - - - - - -   100

Trip No.   *Page*

47 MCKENZIE RIVER - - - - - - - - - 102
48 PAMELIA LAKE - - - - - - - - - - 104
49 MIDDLE FORK WILLAMETTE - - - - - - 105

Part Six
SOUTHERN OREGON

50 LAKE OF THE WOODS - - - - - - - - 109
51 UPPER ROGUE - - - - - - - - - - 111
52 MIDDLE ROGUE - - - - - - - - - - 113
53 APPLEGATE RIVER - - - - - - - - - 115
54 ILLINOIS RIVER - - - - - - - - 117
55 NORTH UMPQUA - - - - - - - - - 119
56 SOUTH UMPQUA - - - - - - - - - 121
57 WILLIAMSON RIVER - - - - - - - - 123
58 KLAMATH LAKE - - - - - - - - - 124
59 KLAMATH RIVER - - - - - - - - - 125
60 ODELL LAKE - - - - - - - - - - 126

Part Seven
DESCHUTES BELT

61 MIDDLE DESCHUTES - - - - - - - - 132
62 LOWER DESCHUTES - - - - - - - - 134
63 WARM SPRINGS RESERVATION - - - - - 136
64 CRANE PRAIRIE AND WICKIUP - - - - - 137
65 EAST AND PAULINA LAKES - - - - - - 139
66 PRINEVILLE RESERVOIR - - - - - - - 141
67 OLALLIE LAKE - - - - - - - - - - 142
68 FALL RIVER - - - - - - - - - - - 144
69 HOSMER LAKE - - - - - - - - - - 145
70 METOLIUS RIVER - - - - - - - - - 147

Part Eight
NORTHEAST OREGON

71 UMATILLA RIVER (lower) - - - - - - 152
72 JOHN DAY ARM - - - - - - - - - 154
73 WENAHA CANYON - - - - - - - - - 156

Trip
No.   Page

74 LOWER GRANDE RONDE - - - - - - -   157
75 CATHERINE CREEK - - - - - - - -   158
76 MAGONE LAKE - - - - - - - - -   159
77 UPPER HELLS CANYON - - - - - - -   161
78 MIDDLE SNAKE - - - - - - - - -   163
79 LOSTINE RIVER - - - - - - - - -   164
80 MINAM RIVER - - - - - - - - -   166
81 UPPER JOHN DAY RIVER - - - - - -   167
82 MIDDLE FORK JOHN DAY - - - - - -   169
83 LOWER IMNAHA—DUG BAR - - - - -   171
84 JUBILEE LAKE - - - - - - - - -   173
85 UPPER UMATILLA RIVER - - - - - -   175
86 SOUTH FORK WALLA WALLA - - - - -   176
87 WALLOWA RIVER - - - - - - - -   177

Part Nine
SOUTHEAST OREGON

88 OWYHEE LAKE - - - - - - - - -   182
89 STRAWBERRY LAKE - - - - - - -   184
90 MALHEUR RESERVOIR - - - - - - -   186
91 FISH LAKE - - - - - - - - - -   187
92 EMIGRANT CREEK - - - - - - - -   189
93 DONNER UND BLITZEN RIVER - - - -   190
94 MANN LAKE - - - - - - - - - -   191
95 COW LAKES - - - - - - - - - -   192

Part Ten
OFFSHORE OREGON

96 CAPE KIWANDA - - - - - - - - -   196
97 BLUE WATER TUNA - - - - - - - -   198
98 COLUMBIA BAR - - - - - - - - -   200
99 DEPOE BAY - - - - - - - - - -   202
100 WINCHESTER BAY - - - - - - - -   204
101 THE STONEWALL BANK - - - - - - -   205

LIST OF ILLUSTRATIONS

Page

South Coast Map 16
New River in the South Coast Country 18
Surf Perch Caught on South Coast 18
Shad Fishing on Millicoma 21
Bill Roberts with Nice Shad 21
Rogue Canyon Wilderness 23
Rogue River Canyon 24
Paradise Bar, Middle Rogue 24
Anglers on the Middle Rogue 28
At the Mouth of the Rogue River 29
Six-and-Half-Pound Black Bass 32
Siltcoos Lake Catch of Bass 32
A Six-Pound Siltcoos Bass 32
Siltcoos Black Bass 32
Bass Fishing is Growing in Oregon 32
The Umpqua River 34
Two Fine Stripers from the Lower Umpqua 37
Guide Denny Hannah with a "Schoolie" 37
North Coast Map 44
Nehalem River and Bay 47
The Pacific Ocean Nehalem Bay 49
Tillamook Bay Bar 51
Town of Garibaldi 51
Winter Steelhead from Nestucca River 52
Nestucca River in Winter 53
A Bottom Fishing Charter Boat 59
Buzz Ramsey and Steelhead 59
The Author with a Nice Steelhead 60
Winter Steelhead 60
Bill Young on the Coquille River 63
Salmon Fishing on the Oregon Coast 64
Map of Columbia River 66, 67
Puget Island in the Lower Columbia 66, 67

Page

Charter Boat Fishing 68
Shad Fishing — Washougal River 70
Sturgeon from off Tongue Point 70
Smallmouth Bass from Middle Columbia 72
Boat Harbor at Hammond, Oregon 72
Art Lacey and Shad 74
"Social Security Beach" 74
Don Holm with Winter Steelhead 75
Steelhead Fishing near Arlington, Oregon 76
The Columbia River West of The Dalles 78
Sturgeon from Lower Columbia 80
Rooster Rock State Park 82
Map of Metropolitan Area 84
Salmon Fishing on the Willamette below the Falls 86
Timothy Lake and Mount Hood 89
The Clackamas River 91
Winter Steelheading on the Clackamas 91
Clackamas River Steelheading 91
Angler at Henry-Hagg Lake 92
Pudding River 94
Sandy River 94
Map of Willamette Watershed 96
Wilsonville Bridge on Willamette River 98
Detroit Lake 100
North Santiam East of Salem 101
Waldo Lake 103
Fisherman on McKenzie River Drift Boat 103
Trout Fishing on McKenzie 103
Upper North Falls, Silver Falls Park 106
Map of Southern Oregon 108
Lake of the Woods 110
Fishing on Rogue above Trail 112
Rogue Rapids 114
Drifting Rogue River White Water 114
Hellgate Canyon 116
Floating the Rogue 118
Lake Selmac 118
Lemolo Falls on North Umpqua 120
Diamond Lake 122
Odell Lake in Cascades 127
Mackinaw Trout from Odell 127

Page

Map of Deschutes Belt 128
Fishing Means Good Eatin' 130-31
Rainbow Catch from Upper Deschutes 133
Deschutes Southwest of Bend, Oregon 133
The Deschutes River near Redmond, Oregon 135
Crane Prairie Reservoir 138
Paulina Lake 140
Brown Trout from East Lake 140
Olallie Lake in High Cascades 143
Fall River in Central Oregon 144
Metolius River and Mount Jefferson 146
Three Creeks Lake 146
Blue Lake near Suttle Lake 146
Map of Northeast Oregon 150-51
The Umatilla River near Bar M Ranch 153
A Nice Smallmouth Bass from John Day River 155
Cathedral Rock and John Day River 160
Grand Canyon of the Snake 162
Moccasin Lake in Eagle Cap 165
The John Day River and Fossil Beds 168
Smallmouth Bass from John Day River 170
Eastern Oregon Crappie 172
Wallowa Falls 174
Aneroid Lake 174
Anthony Lakes 178
Bear Lake 178
Wallowa Lake 178
Map of Southeast Oregon 180-81
Owyhee Lake 183
The Owyhee Canyon and River 183
Strawberry Mountain Area 185
Strawberry Lake 185
Kiger Canyon in the Steens Mountain 188
Owyhee Lake 189
Black Crappie from Owyhee Lake 193
Owyhee River Canyon 193
Maps of Offshore Fishing Ports 194
Offshore Salmon 197
Fighting and Albacore Far Offshore 197
Albacore in the Net 199
Salmon On! 201

Page

Salmon Catch off the Columbia River 201
Landing a Fightin' Albacore 203
Rockfish Caught off Coos Bay 206
The Author and a Catch of "Toothy Critters" 206
Off the Coast of Oregon at Sunrise in a Dory 207

INTRODUCTION

Where's a good place to go fishin'?

Almost every day someone greets me with this question. In fact, it's not so much an inquiry as it is a salutation like *How's she goin'?* or *How're ya feelin'?* The greeter doesn't really care how she's goin' or how you are feelin'.

But in the case of *Where's a good place to go fishin'?* often as not they really do want to know, and they believe I can tell them because I am Wildlife Editor of *The Oregonian*, as well as a freelance writer on outdoor subjects.

Moreover, during the spring, summer, and fall I get numerous telephone calls and letters from New York, Washington, D.C., and Miami, Florida, from folks who have heard about Oregon's fine fishing and are planning a trip out this way.

So I have persuaded myself that there is a need for a convenient book that tells where there is a good spot to go fishing, in simple form without a lot of extraneous information probably already known or easily picked up along the way; a book that will pinpoint for the fisherman —whether a stranger or a local resident who doesn't have an opportunity to scout out good spots for himself—some trips I think he'd enjoy taking.

For the benefit of visitors: Oregon has 96,981 square miles of elbow room, including 666 square miles of water surface, and 429 miles of Pacific Ocean coastline (nearly 400 of which are in public ownership), ranging from sea level to about 12,000-feet elevation; with a terrain that varies from coastal rain forests and lush green interior valleys to snowcapped mountain ranges, lava rimrocks, and sagebrush deserts.

Oregon has hundreds of lakes, thousands of miles of river frontage, and 80,000 miles of highways and roads to provide access. About fifty percent of the state is still in public ownership—federal, state, and county lands— so there is yet plenty of room to roam.

In all of its thirty-six counties there are only two million people, or about twenty people per square mile. And about half these people annually buy hunting and fishing licenses.

I would estimate that there are between 5,000 and 10,000 fishing "holes" in Oregon. Therefore, boiling these down to the best 101 fishing trips was a difficult chore. As the recruit sorting spuds on KP duty said, it wasn't the work that hurt—it was making all those decisions.

In the final selection I had to leave out some of my favorite spots, such as the remote *Narrows* on the John Day, beautiful Frances Lake in the Wallowas, the superb little family spot, Lake Selmac in Josephine County, and many others for one reason or another. I also probably left out some favorites of other folks, and no doubt will hear about it.

But the ones remaining, I believe, most nearly include all the elements that must be considered, such as variety, geographic and seasonal variations, best prospects for a successful trip, kind of tackle and gear needed, and method of fishing. I also considered such things as historical interest, scenic beauty, and simply esthetic value —for angling, if nothing else, is perhaps less of a "sport" than it is a total outdoor experience, an escape *back* into sensual reality.

In each case I have also included one or more alternate spots in the same general area. Need I say that the best fishing holes have their off days also?

The sites have also been selected as much as possible for the angler with only one fishing outfit. It is my personal belief that one rod, one line, and one lure, will catch any game fish in Oregon (although there isn't much point in proving it).

Finally, these are the places I would (and frequently do) choose when I go fishing for fun instead of a story.

Maybe I'll see you at one of them soon.

Introduction to Third Edition

Twenty-one years have passed since the original publication of this book, eleven years since the second edition revisions. In the outdoors field, and particularly in sport fishing, many changes have taken place—not only in the management of these resources, but in the public's attitude. Most people now accept the philosophy of angling for the pleasure of the experience, instead of the meat. They now accept quality fishing rather than bringing home a creel full.

Most of the changes in fish management have been in the anadromous species—such as salmon and steelhead that spend their lives in the open sea and run into the rivers to spawn. These species have been under heavy pressure for the past three decades from commercial and Indian overfishing, from poaching by foreign vessels, and by political interference. It is unlikely that we will ever experience the fabulous salmon fishing off the Columbia River. Those days live only in the memory and scrapbooks of big catches of forty-pound chinooks. Gone, too, are the big salmon derbies.

There is a ray of hope, however. Modern management practices are bringing back the runs in some of the old favorites, such as the Rogue, the Willamette, the Clackamas and the Coos. Perhaps our children will someday get a taste of the way it once was.

And for the rest of the trips described in this book, you will find conditions pretty much as they were when first reported. Regulations change year by year, and so do guide services, and accommodations, but the streams, lakes, and old fishin' holes are still there, waiting for you.

D.H.

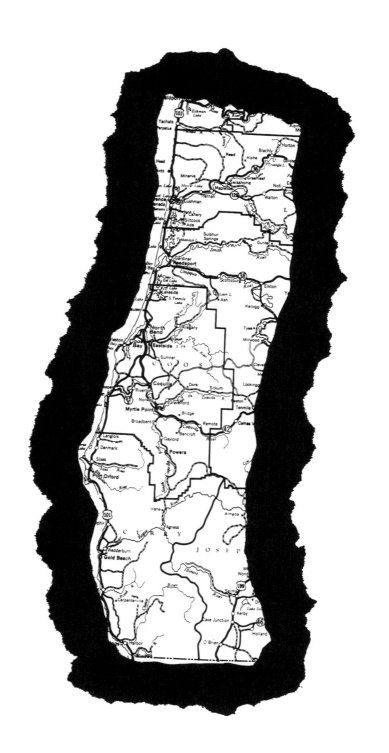

PART I

SOUTH COAST

Don Holm Photo

"NEW RIVER" IN THE SOUTH COAST COUNTRY

Don Holm Photo

SURF PERCH CAUGHT ON SOUTH COAST

Trip No. 1

Alternates:
   Floras Lake
   Sixes River
   Pacific Ocean

New River
Curry County
Coos County

A caravan of cars drove south along U.S. 101. Friends were taking me surfperch fishing, and we could have dropped off anywhere along this south coast of Oregon, but they had a favorite spot. A few miles south of Bandon we turned right on an obscure side road and wound through the madrone, coastal pine, and salal for a couple of miles until we came to a delightful picnic spot on the banks of New River.

New River is a short freshwater stream that drains several dunes lakes. We pulled on waders and forded the shallow stream, then hiked over the dunes to the beach. Rigging up ordinary spinning outfits, using two-ounce pyramid sinkers and a two-hook set-up with number 6 hooks baited with small pieces of clam neck, we cast into the first line of surf. A sharp strike, a powerful struggle, and in came a pretty little redtail perch. We caught them so fast that it took two men to keep up with the filleting. We didn't bother cleaning them; just cut the two fillets off. Panfried, perch are super delicious.

This spot is only one of many along the three hundred miles of almost deserted Oregon beaches that await the explorations of surf fishermen.

Trip No. 2   Millicoma River Shad
                                 Coos County

Alternates:
   Coos River
   Umpqua River
   Rogue River

The Millicoma is another name for the North Fork Coos, coming down through a deep slash in the rugged Coast Range and joining the main Coos just east of the city of Coos Bay. It is largely unknown to sports anglers, except for local people who fish it all year around for shad, sea-run cutthroat, striped bass, salmon, and steelhead.

Most of the shad and striped bass fishing is done from boats trolling upriver from the junction. The best time for the sporty shad (as well as the striped bass) is during the spawning period in the early spring.

Here's the way Dr. Al Buck, Vince Aleksa, Bill Roberts, and guide Doug Crawford do it: Troll slowly with a small brass, copper, or silver wobbler, with a leader weighted just enough to run close to the bottom, and about fifty feet behind the boat. This means frequent snag-ups, but also fish. The best time is on the change of the tide.

But the most exciting time is just before dark when the shad rise to the surface. That's when you have a ball, as the frenzied shad slash and rip back and forth across the river, around the boat, up and downstream, in their mysterious spawning rites. Sometimes the shad and striped bass (both exotics imported to the Pacific from the Atlantic) will be spawning at the same time. Then they take any kind of surface lure. And this is when the excitement of fishing is the most "catching."

BILL ROBERTS *(foreground)* SHAD FISHING ON THE
MILLICOMA RIVER

BILL ROBERTS WITH A NICE SHAD

Trip No. 3   Striped Bass Country
                                    Coos County
Alternates: *Douglas County*
   Umpqua River
   Smith River
   Coos River

The striped bass is an old favorite with East Coast saltwater anglers, to say nothing of Californians who find them throughout the Sacramento system where they were first introduced in the 1870s.

Striped bass are also found in great numbers in Oregon's coastal streams such as the Coos, Smith, and Umpqua rivers. Many of these are known to be record-breaking fish, but for reasons difficult to understand, Oregonians look down their noses at these superb game-fish. Therefore, those who do go for stripers have the sport all to themselves.

One of the best trips for stripers is to the lower Umpqua at Reedsport on the coast highway, U.S. 101. There are several tackle stores, and a number of rental docks, and even guide services can be arranged. The best time of the year is through the winter months, although exact times are unpredictable. Late spring, when the stripers are spawning, is probably the best time of all.

Surface plugs such as the Rebel work well, as do deep-trolled eels and similar lures. Heavy salmon tackle is needed, since the stripers range all the way from ten or fifteen pounds up to sixty or seventy pounds. Besides, you might also accidentally hook up with a huge sturgeon.

Trip No. 4   Lower Rogue
                           Curry County
Alternates:
None

The Rogue is one of the world's most famous rivers, stamping ground of movie stars, admirals, generals, presidents and vice presidents, merchant princes, for more than a hundred years. The best way to get acquainted with the Rogue is just to let it happen to you.

It is generally divided into three parts, like Gaul: the lower river from the ocean at Gold Beach to Agness, end of the road; the middle or wilderness section from Agness to Galice, the historic old mining camp; and the upper river through Grants Pass and the interior valleys to its headwaters in the Cascades near Crater Lake.

The lower section is boatable most of the year, and

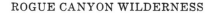

ROGUE CANYON WILDERNESS
Don Holm Photo

guides and jetboat service are readily available at Gold Beach and Wedderburn. Here offshore charter boats are also available. Campsites, boat ramps, "salmon boards," and plunking spots are many up both sides of the river to Lobster Creek.

You can fish the jetties all year 'round for ocean fish; trout during trout season; shad in early spring; steelhead and salmon from early spring until winter. The steelhead fly fishing is terrific in early fall. Rogue River chinook salmon is rated the best eating of all. What more could one ask?

Don Holm Photo

ROGUE RIVER CANYON

MIDDLE ROGUE RIVER, CANYON WILDERNESS

Don Holm Photo

Trip No. 5   Hunter Creek
                                  Curry County

Alternates:
  Pistol River
  Chetco River

A small fragile stream that has a remarkable run of fish. It is stocked heavily with rainbow and cuts, but has some excellent sea-run fly fishing in the fall. Also the steelheading around the first of the year is excellent. The coho and chinook salmon are in about October and November and early December.

There is a road a short way up the creek, but also considerable private land. Always ask permission. Bank plunking is the *modus operandi*.

There is a tavern in the town at the highway crossing, in case you get skunked upriver. Accommodations and services are available in Gold Beach just north on U.S. 101.

Hunter Creek is noted for the rapidity with which it clears up after heavy rain, so don't despair if it looks muddy at first.

Trip No. 6

Pistol River
Curry County

Alternates:
Rogue River
Hunter Creek

This small tortuous river drops down into the ocean out of the wild coast mountains through the settlement of Pistol River, just south of Gold Beach. There is a logging road up about ten miles. In places the driving is quite hairy and the real estate is all vertical.

Pistol River is a good trout, steelhead, and salmon stream, but being only about fifteen miles long, does not support a large fishery. It is stocked with rainbow and cutthroat, and also has a run of harvest trout or bluebacks in the late summer and fall. Some steelhead are caught early in the year. October and November are the salmon months, with fair coho and chinook fishing in November.

Not a good boating river, but bank plunking is the most productive method anyway.

Accommodations are limited at the river.

Generally, the waters below U.S. 101 to the ocean are closed at various times, so the angling synopsis should be carefully checked for closures and special regulations.

Trip No. 7   Winchuck River
                                    Curry County
Alternates:
    Smith River
    Klamath River

Winchuck River is in Oregon, but during a hot salmon run California fishermen outnumber the natives. At times like this, smart Oregonians go down into California and fish the Smith and Klamath.

A pretty little stream, there is none other like Winchuck in Oregon. This small, fragile river enters the ocean almost on the border. The lower section is an excellent drift stream, and the salmon pour in when the first rains hit. Its total length is about fifteen miles, and there is some private posted property on it.

Winchuck is well-stocked with rainbow and cutthroat, but the trout fishing is good only in the spring and fall. It is a good winter steelhead river in January, but the run of course is a small one. The coho and chinooks are there in November and December.

You can get supplies and services at Harbor, Brookings, and various other communities. There are a number of state parks and campgrounds on both sides of the border.

Don Holm Photo

A HAPPY GROUP OF ANGLERS ON THE MIDDLE ROGUE

Trip No. 8   Chetco River
                                Curry County
Alternates:
  Rogue River
  Illinois River

Chetco River is one of my favorites, although if pressed I could not tell you why. About forty miles long, with its head up in the rugged Kalmiopsis Wilderness of the Siskiyous, the Chetco is a remarkable fishery. At the mouth and in the harbor (Brookings), there's a booming saltwater sports center with charter boats and all the usual services for salmon and bottom fishing.

Upstream there are numerous salmon and steelhead "holes" that are fishable during the fall and winter rains.

The river is heavily stocked with rainbow and cut-throat. The trout fishing is excellent in early season and again in late summer and fall for sea-runs.

Steelheading is in December and January, coho and chinook salmon from August through October.

It is accessible from Brookings on U.S. 101, where there are a number of state parks and campgrounds. Boating the river for the first fifteen or twenty miles is perhaps the easier course. A road up the river gets progressively worse and much of the land is in private ownership and posted. Since there is heavy pressure on this river from "outsiders," some of these landowners are easily aroused.

SALMON FISHING AT THE MOUTH OF THE ROGUE RIVER

Photo Courtesy Oregon State Highway Travel Division

Trip No. 9

Siuslaw Bay
Lane County

Alternates:
   Ocean beaches
   Local lakes

In recent years the small estuary which collects the Siuslaw before dumping into the ocean near Florence has become a bright spot in the salmon fishing picture on the Central Coast. The Siuslaw bar used to be almost impassable, but jetties and dredging have made it safe during good weather.

The offshore fishing is good all summer, and the bay is also a good producer then. However, late summer and fall are the best times inside.

Some really big chinook have been taken here in the fall. The late summer sea-run cutthroat fishing is also excellent. Jack salmon fishing is good about the same time. The coho and chinook come in about August. Winter steelheading starts in late fall.

Also in the bay are clams, crabs, flounder, and perch. On the beach side there is surf fishing.

The Siuslaw Port has a boat ramp and harbor, and all facilities are available locally. The quaint waterfront is as yet undiscovered by the average tourist.

Trip No. 10   Siltcoos Lake
                               Lane County

Alternates:
   Tahkenitch Lake
   Carter Lake

Siltcoos is Oregon's "bass country," and at this writing holds the record for the state with a largemouth of 9½ pounds. Without doubt the lake contains ten-pound-plus bass, but so far no one has been able to outsmart them.

The lake is a large one, with several islands, and a wooded, hilly shoreline, nestled between the coast mountains and the ocean. There is a railroad on the east shore, which also runs south around Tahkenitch Lake, another top bass and panfish spot. Paved or gravel roads give access to most of the Siltcoos. The lake is about halfway between Florence and Reedsport and easy to miss since the turn-off on U.S. 101 is obscure. The principal access roads lead to Westlake, and to North Shore Road and Booth Arm. There are several resorts with cottages, boat rentals, and all facilities. Also in the neighborhood are several good state parks and forest campgrounds. The ocean is just over the wooded dunes from Siltcoos.

Siltcoos not only has some superb bass fishing, but also perch, crappies, bluegills, catfish, native trout and sea-run cutthroat, steelhead, and an astonishing coho salmon run. In fact, the *Field & Stream* coho record one year came out of Siltcoos. There isn't a month out of the year when the lake cannot be fished for something.

Don Holm Photo

A SIX-POUND SILTCOOS BASS

Don Holm Photo

A SILTCOOS BLACK BASS

BASS FISHING IS A FAST GROWING ACTIVITY IN OREGON

Don Holm Photo

Trip No. 11   Lower Umpqua
                               Douglas County
Alternates:
    Lower Smith River
    Winchester Bay

The lower Umpqua up to tidewater is a remarkable fishery, one of the best in the country. At various times it contains striped bass, shad, steelhead, salmon, sturgeon, sea-run cuts, catfish, and native trout. There are few times during the year when you cannot enjoy some kind of fishing, and many times when it is exciting beyond belief—such as when the striped bass are spawning on the surface and taking surface plugs at night.

World record striped bass, sturgeon, and salmon have come from this river, and each year it seems to get better, not worse. For one thing, the comprehensive steelhead and salmon management programs for the upper river are making progress in spite of pollution and over-population.

The Umpqua here is reached at Reedsport on U.S. 101, and State 38 runs up the south bank all the way to Elkton, with other roads to Roseburg and upper reaches. The Umpqua's neighboring river, the Smith, which comes into the bay nearby, is also a superb fishing stream, although smaller than the Big U.

Salmon fishing starts in early spring, and peaks again in the fall. There are runs of both summer and winter steelhead. The shad appear in the spring. Trout fishing is all year 'round; so is sturgeon. Stripers in spring and fall.

THE UMPQUA RIVER ALONG STATE HIGHWAY 38 IN OREGON

Trip No. 12   Tenmile Lakes
                               Coos County
Alternates:
   Tenmile Outlet
   Coos River

Tenmile Lakes are a string of jewel-like lakes between the wooded coastal mountains and the ocean sand dunes. The principal fishing waters are South Tenmile and North Tenmile. These lakes were treated in 1968 to eliminate trash fish, and replanted with rainbow trout. For a couple of years, the lakes were the hottest trout fishing on the West Coast. Then they went bad again, mainly because the trout could not stand the pressure and somebody had once again illegally introduced spiny ray species. This ruined the trout fishery, for a time anyway.

The Oregon Fish and Wildlife Department next dumped in a heavy plant of largemouth black bass to control the bluegills. The result became one of the best bass and bluegill waters in the west. This is an all-year fishery, but the best bass fishing is in the spring.

In the fall, Tenmile Creek which empties into the ocean, is a good steelhead and coho stream. During mayfly hatches in spring and summer, the lakes are also fair flyfishing for trout. Sea-run cutthroat appear in the outlet in late summer.

South Tenmile is the largest, about 1,500 acres; North Tenmile is about 1,000 acres. Access is from U.S. 101 about ten miles north of Coos Bay. Stores, motels, bait shops, boat rentals, and public launch ramp are located at Lakeside, a little community on South Tenmile. A state landing strip is also located adjacent.

Trip No. 13   Coos River
                               Coos County
Alternates:
  Millicoma
  South Fork

Very few people, except for locals, fish the Coos River. Most don't know where it is, how to get to it, what fish are there, or how to catch them. A short river system which falls sharply out of the rugged coast mountains, it's only about twenty miles long, but has two major forks —the North or Millicoma, and the South Fork—as well as a small West Fork. The Millicoma and the South Fork come together just above Eastside, reached by county road around the south end of the Bay. The road up the South Fork ends at Dellwood, a popular fishing spot. The road up the Millicoma goes to Allegany, Myrtle Grove, Gold and Silver Falls park and loops around Elk Peak to Loon Lake and the Umpqua River below Scottsburg.

Most fishing is done from boats, but there are a number of bank plunking spots in spite of the extensive private lands. Local information is needed for best fishing times, but generally the striped bass run in spring and fall, the shad in the spring (at the same time as bass), the steelhead in December and January, sea-run cuts in the late summer, chinook and coho salmon in late fall and early winter, native trout all year.

Local services and guides are available in Coos Bay, and strangers should go with a guide the first time.

Don Holm Photo

GUIDE DENNY HANNAH WITH A "SCHOOLIE"

Don Holm Photo

TWO FINE STRIPERS FROM LOWER UMPQUA RIVER

Trip No. 14   Coos Bay
Coos County

Alternates:
  Coos River
  Ocean Beaches

A major West Coast harbor, and one of the largest lumber ports in the world, Coos Bay is also a remarkable sport fishing center all year around, with several runs of salmon, steelhead, striped bass, shad, sea-run cutthroat, plus crabbing and clamming on the flats, and bottom fishing from the jetties and just outside the bar on the reefs for halibut, lingcod, perch, greenling, and rockfish of all kinds.

Just inside the bar, at Charleston, there is a new, modern small-boat harbor with all services and a considerable charter fleet. The outside salmon fishing season runs from May to October. Some boats also go out from here to the albacore waters offshore.

The shad move into the bay in early spring, although bay fishing for them is not considered good. The striped bass are in and out of the bay most of the year, but are not fished for much until they move into the rivers, with the best fishing in early spring and fall.

There are also sturgeon in the bay and tidewater areas, although few people fish for them.

Boat rentals, guide services, and complete accommodations are available around the bay.

Trip No. 15

Alternates:
  North Fork
  Middle Fork
  East Fork
  South Fork

Coquille River
Coos County
Curry County
Douglas County

The Coquille is a major coastal river and one of the best in the Northwest, although greatly underrated and unappreciated even by local folks. It enters the Pacific at Bandon, where there is an excellent harbor with a good offshore and bay fishery in late summer and fall. The main river heads in rugged mountain country just west of Roseburg; the North Fork on across the divide from the Coos River east of Coos Bay; the Middle Fork in Camas Valley, a pleasant section on State 42 southwest of Roseburg; and the South Fork in the wild Rogue River mountains around Marial and Mt. Bolivar.

The principal towns or settlements on the watershed are Bandon, Myrtle Point, Coquille, Powers, Remote, Riverton, and Prosper.

Fishing includes striped bass in summer and fall; salmon through November; winter and summer runs of steelhead; harvest trout or cutthroat in the late summer and fall; plus shad in the spring; native rainbow and cuts all year, catfish, perch, flounder, crabs, and so on.

There are numerous campgrounds, boat ramps, and other facilities and services at most points, and it is a mystery why this river system doesn't get more play.

Trip No. 16   Elk River
                               Curry County

Alternates:
  Pacific Ocean
  Sixes River

The Elk River enters the ocean just north of Cape Blanco and is crossed by U.S. 101. There are good roads along much of the river and considerable private land, but this is one of the best streams on the South Coast for salmon, steelhead, and trout. It is also the site of a new modern salmon hatchery, built largely with federal funds, which will eventually boost the sport and commercial fisheries in this part of the state.

The trout fishing for cutthroat mostly is best in the spring and fall. There is a run of harvest trout after the fall rains. Salmon fishing is open only from spring until about December 1st, but dates vary and the regulations should be checked. The chinook and coho fishing is excellent in tidewater in October and November. The steelheading is good after the fall rains, continuing through December, with January and February best. The deadline for winter fishing is about eleven miles up from the ocean.

Services and accommodations are available along U. S. 101, and there is a fine state park camping facility at Humbug Mountain.

Trip No. 17   Sixes River
                               Curry County
Alternates:
  Elk River
  New River

The Sixes is a favorite of mine—maybe just because I'm intrigued with the name, which, incidentally, is derived from the Indian word *Sik-ses-tene*, corrupted to Sixes by the 1855 miners.

The river is located north of Port Orford and south of Bandon, a good coastal stream that gets very low in summer but is a first class harvest trout, steelhead, and salmon stream. It is heavily planted with trout, with trout fishing good only summer and fall.

When the fall rains start, all hell breaks loose as the sea-run cuts, coho and chinook salmon, and winter steelhead move in from the ocean. Steelheading is best in December and January; salmon fishing October, November.

Salmon fishing is closed above Dry Creek, and there is a steelhead deadline about ten miles up. Check the regs carefully. Note also a closure at the mouth through the winter season. Surf fishing, incidentally, is excellent along here, too.

Camping facilities, supplies, services, and accommodations are available all along U.S. 101, which crosses the Sixes.

Trip No. 18   Siuslaw River
                               Lane County
Alternates:
   Siuslaw Bay

The rugged, one-hundred-mile-long Siuslaw River heads in the mountains south of Eugene, is joined by Wolf Creek, and then Lake Creek draining Triangle Lake, and plunges through some of Oregon's wildest real estate to come out in the bay at Florence.

This river is hard to fish above tidewater, but has top runs of steelhead and salmon, to say nothing of bluebacks or harvest trout or sea-run cuts. There is some good native trout fishing as well, and some good fly fishing water. Lake Creek is a wild one and has some excellent steelhead and coho fishing. The best action for sea-run species is from August through January.

Facilities and campsites are limited above tidewater. Access is not too easy. State highways 36 and 126 follow the stream fairly close and connect with U.S. 101 at Florence and U.S. 99 near Eugene.

Trip No. 19   Vulcan Lake
                               Curry County
Alternates:
  Chetco River

A fishing trip to Vulcan Lake is one of the "strangest" in the entire country. Vulcan is a small lake of about thirty acres just inside the remote and somewhat weird Kalmiopsis Wilderness at the headwaters of the Chetco. The lake itself is at the northeast foot of Vulcan Peak, which is more than 4,200-feet high. Vulcan (and a smaller unnamed lake nearby) is one of the sources of the Chetco, flowing down Box Canyon Creek and into the river near Taggarts Bar.

These lakes and the creek are good trout fishing but can be reached only by trail through some of the ruggedest country on the continent, the best access being up the Chetco from Brookings by road to the beginning of the trail in the Vulcan Peak area.

The Kalmiopsis is a 76,200-acre wilderness, little known even to local people, embracing a harsh, broken region, with deep gorges and rugged outcroppings, dense forests and a stark unreal beauty. It was first penetrated by the 1850 gold prospectors, and some of their remains are still there. The geology goes back to the Mesozoic age, is highly mineralized and contains many unique "living fossils" only recently discovered and known to exist nowhere else in the world. These include the rare Brewer spruce, the carnivorous Darlingtonia plant, Jeffrey pines, Leachiana—as well as "modern" wildlife and flora.

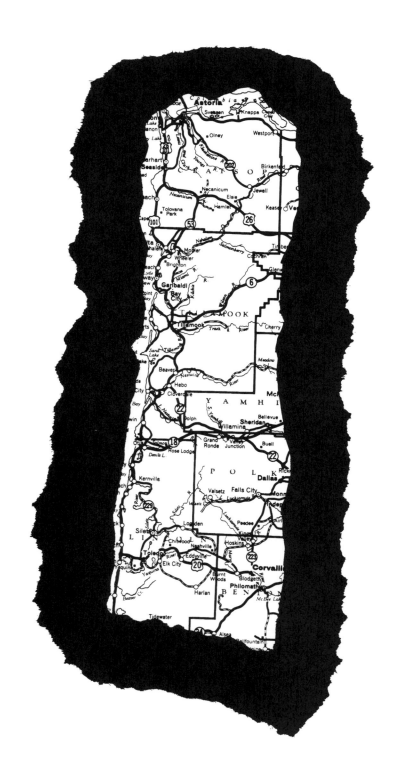

PART II

NORTH COAST

Trip No. 20   Nehalem River
                               Tillamook County
Alternates: *Clatsop County*
  Tillamook Bay   *Columbia County*
  Necanicum River

The Nehalem heads on the divide separating the rich
Tualatin Valley from the coastal region in the vicinity
of Vernonia. It flows through logged-over forest land,
stump ranches, old homesteads, and modern farms. During
the hot summer the upper reaches often become a
series of connected pools. Below the old stagecoach station
of Elsie, the Nehalem takes on respectability, and
picking up the Salmonberry it becomes a major river that
once supported some of the best salmon and steelhead
fishing in the world.

Boating the Nehalem is a popular way of fishing.
However, a road also follows its course most of the way
from Elsie. A highly productive spot is around the Salmonberry.

The North Fork Nehalem flows from north to south,
almost parallel with the coastline, through logged-over
land that looks like something the devil has wrought. It
has a new coho hatchery, and an attempt finally is being
made to rehabilitate the salmon runs. It is also stocked
with rainbow and cutthroat and has a good steelhead run
in December. The North Fork now has better spawning
waters than the Nehalem but is not nearly so large a
stream.

The Nehalem is accessible in most places by U.S. 26
and State 202; the North Fork by State 53.

Photo Courtesy Oregon State Highway Travel Division

NEHALEM RIVER AND BAY, TWENTY-FIVE MILES SOUTH OF SEASIDE

Trip No. 21   Nehalem Bay
                                  Tillamook County

Alternates:
   North Fork
   Nehalem River

A very fine estuary, Nehalem Bay is coming into its own again after falling on bad times. The bar here is not what I consider either safe or predictable, but the fishing inside is excellent for saltwater species, for salmon and for sea-runs, and, to a lesser degree, for steelhead.

It is a favorite spot for families who like to take their boat or rent one locally, go across to the sand spit and have a picnic. They put out crab pots, do a little trolling, and even dig a few clams. It's like a saltwater smorgasbord.

The bay receives the water of the North Fork and the main Nehalem, one of the longest of the coast streams. Due to pollution, heavy agricultural use, and some political problems, the main Nehalem has sharply declined as a game fishing stream. Potentially, however, this is a watershed second only to the Rogue and Umpqua.

Photo Courtesy Oregon State Highway Travel Division

THE PACIFIC OCEAN WITH NEHALEM BAY IN THE
BACKGROUND

Trip No. 22
Tillamook Bay
Tillamook County

Alternates:
Wilson River
Trask River
Nestucca River
Netarts Bay

Largest estuary on the Oregon coast, Tillamook Bay has everything in the saltwater line, plus the Trask, Tillamook, Wilson, Miami, and Kilchis rivers—all of them excellent steelhead, salmon, and sea-run cutthroat streams. The Game Commission has been active here with its winter steelhead program and has an experimental super-chinook salmon program going too. Check the *Synopsis* for local regulations on anadromous species.

The bay also has some fine crabbing, clamming, and fishing for perch, flounder, and halibut all year 'round. The entrance or bar is located near Garibaldi, where you can get an offshore charter boat, rent a boat, or fish from the jetties. The city of Tillamook also provides complete services and accommodations.

Fish the tributary rivers during general trout season for natives, in late fall and early autumn for sea-run cuts, in the fall and winter for salmon and steelhead. Salmon fishing in the bay is good in August and September, offshore in June, July, August, and September. Inside the bay the best salmon fishing is from the Coast Guard to the Ghost Hole.

TILLAMOOK BAY BAR

Don Holm Photo

THE TOWN OF GARIBALDI ON TILLAMOOK BAY

Photo Courtesy Oregon State Highway Travel Division

Trip No. 23   Nestucca River
                               Tillamook County
Alternates:
   There is no
   substitute for
   the Ol' Nestuck!

Everything that moves into Nestucca Bay, also moves up into the tidewater reaches of the Nestucca River, a fairly long coastal river as coast rivers go. Above tidewater also are native rainbow and cutthroat, with the best trout fishing in the spring and fall. During the summer the upper river often dries up to a series of connected pools.

The river heads in the rugged, almost inaccessible Coast Range just north and west of McMinnville. I have seen and photographed its source, but it wasn't easy. Several years ago an old dam, privately owned by a fishing club, burst after a quarter century of blocking the

WINTER STEELHEAD FROM THE NESTUCCA RIVER

Don Holm Photo

Don Holm Photo

NESTUCCA RIVER IN WINTER

upper section and improved the upper spawning beds. However, the city of McMinnville then built a water supply dam just above it, so the river is still barred in the extreme headwaters.

Downstream, however, some of the finest winter steelheading in the land occurs in November and December. The chinook and coho also move into the river in the fall and early winter. No motors are allowed in winter, but drifting is the best way to fish it. There are many bank plunking spots available, although much of the river bank is private.

Harvest trout fishing with flies or bait is excellent, and so is jack salmon fishing in the late summer and fall. Guides, boats, supplies are all readily available.

Trip No. 24   Nestucca Bay
                               Tillamook County
Alternates:
    Neskowin Creek
    Little Nestucca River
    Nestucca River
    Sand Lake

My all-time favorite spot on the Oregon coast, Nestucca Bay receives the waters of the Little Nestucca—a short, hard-to-fish, but good steelhead and salmon river —as well as the Ol' Nestuck itself.

The Bay is located on a loop road off U.S. 101, about twenty miles south of Tillamook. On its shores are the fishing village of Pacific City, a state-maintained airstrip, and close by some twenty miles of the finest beaches in Oregon.

In the bay you can clam, crab, and fish for sea-run cuts in the autumn, for native trout during the season, for perch, flounder, chinook and coho salmon, jack salmon, and even a run of chum salmon, which few people know about. And, of course, there are the famed Nestucca winter steelhead that run to trophy size.

Alongshore, outside the bay, are all manner of marine game fishes such as halibut, flounder, perch, cod, snapper, and rockfish. Under the lee of Cape Kiwanda nearby is the home of the famed dory fleet. Tidewater reaches up the Nestucca as far as Cloverdale.

Boat rentals, motels, services, and supplies are available year around.

The bar is not navigable.

Trip No. 25   Devils Lake
                        Lincoln County
Alternates:
    Salmon River
    Siletz Bay
    Surf Fishing

Connected to the Pacific Ocean by the "shortest river in the world," the D River, Devils Lake is a very fine freshwater lake located in the logged-over forest land along U.S. 101 at the terminus of State 18 from the interior valleys. It is on a commercial stretch of resorts, hamburger joints, motels, roadside zoos, curio shops, and other Coney Island-type facilities known as the "20 Miracle Miles," which incorporates most of the development from Devils Lake to Depoe Bay. Devils Lake itself is surrounded by real estate development but has several public campgrounds and boat launch ramps. The lake has been called the "fastest water" in the world by small-boat racers.

It is one of the best fishing lakes in Oregon, with channel catfish and some superb rainbow trout fishing all year 'round. At one time it was a good largemouth bass lake. Best fishing is by bobber and worm, and often by trolling for trout.

The former towns of Delake and Oceanlake are now part of the conglomerate called Lincoln City. All services are available.

Devils Lake is one place you can go when you can't catch fish anywhere else. However, at this writing the lake is suffering from pollution.

Don Holm Photo

CUTTHROAT TROUT FROM DEVIL'S LAKE ON THE NORTH COAST

Trip No. 26

Alternates:
Siletz Bay
Drift Creek

Siletz River
Lincoln County
Polk County

One of Oregon's best coastal rivers, the Siletz heads in the rugged, forested mountains around Valsetz about twenty miles as the seagull flies from the ocean, but it travels a tortuous one-hundred-mile journey to get there. Euchre Creek is the main tributary. The upper sections are in private tree farms which are not open to the public.

The Game Commission has an intensive steelhead program going in the upper Siletz and it looks as though in the future it will be a top winter and summer steelhead stream, and a fine steelhead fly fishing spot. There are many local regulations and exceptions, so check the *Synopsis* carefully.

The Siletz is also an excellent harvest trout stream and has goodly numbers of jack salmon of which one may take ten a day after September 1. Salmon fishing begins in August, steelheading in November. Ocean perch, flounder, and cod can be caught as far up as the Kernville bridge. There are some native trout in the river, too. Best fishing is by boat, but there are many bank plunking spots and good camping facilities.

Trip No. 27   The Siletz Jaws
                               Lincoln County
Alternates:
   Siletz Bay
   Siletz River

It was September, 1950, and there was a touch of autumn in the air. The line of bank plunkers on the beach at the mouth of the Siletz near Taft (now part of Lincoln City) snickered with contempt when I sat down on a log to assemble my fishing gear. The spinning gear I carried was a radical and controversial innovation, and the colorful saltwater salmon flies were unknown on the Oregon coast. (I had picked them up on Vancouver Island, where coho fly fishing in the salt chuck was an established institution.)

I rigged up my newfangled seven-foot glass spinning rod and to my five-pound test line I tied a blue-and-white coho streamer made of polar bear hair, which is best for salt water. Then I pinched on a little lead about eighteen inches up the line.

The tide was running out. I cast across the current and let the fly swing in an arc. *Wham!* I had a coho on. Ten minutes later, assisted by the wave action, I had it on the beach at my feet. Again I cast and again I had a coho on.

In those days, two was the limit, so I picked up my twelve- and fourteen-pound fish, packed up and left a crowd of bug-eyed, speechless, old-time plunkers wondering what had happened.

As the old mail order ad used to say, "They laughed when I sat down, but when I started to play . . . !"

THE AUTHOR WITH A NICE
STEELHEAD ON COAST
RIVER

Don Holm Photo

A PAIR OF WINTER STEELHEAD WITH ROE FROM THE
SILETZ RIVER

Don Holm Photo

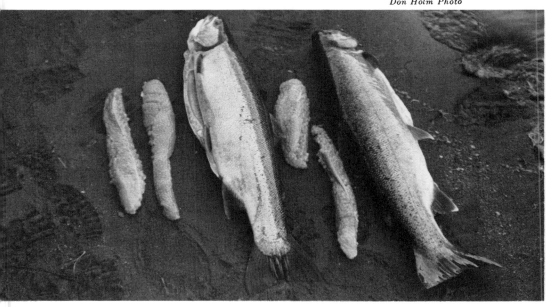

A BOTTOM FISHING CHARTER BOAT RETURNING WITH A
LOAD TO DEPOE BAY

BUZZ RAMSEY AND TWO NICE WINTER STEELHEAD

Trip No. 28   Yaquina Bay
                               Lincoln County
Alternates:
   Yaquina River
   Siletz River

The principal estuary and harbor on the Central Coast, Yaquina is the home of the OSU Marine Science Center, the commercial fishing fleet, and the headquarters for an extensive sport charter fleet. It has a good harbor, a relatively safe bar, some beautiful state parks, and the busy city of Newport.

While offshore salmon fishing has its ups and downs at Yaquina, the bottom fishing is excellent all year over the underwater piles and seamounts. In addition, crabbing and clamming are tops, and there is some surf fishing south of the bay.

Bay fishing includes chinook and coho salmon during the summer and fall runs, harvest trout from August to October, herring jigging, flounder, perch and others.

The bay is bridged by U.S. 101 and can be reached from the interior valleys via U.S. 20 from Corvallis.

The waterfront is a bustling one, colorful and picturesque, and offers all manner of sea-goin' and sport fishing services and supplies, including a number of canneries. Definitely a place to go for fishing or fun.

Trip No. 29   Alsea River
                                 Lincoln County
Alternates:
    Yachats River
    Ocean Beaches
    Alsea Bay

One of Oregon's prettiest streams, the Alsea River with its main tributaries, the North Fork and the South Fork, drains some of the State's most interesting country. Heading up in the wooded foothill country of Benton County, the Alsea cuts through the Coast Range, coming out at Waldport on U.S. 101 and dumps into the ocean. The bar is not navigable but is a popular bank plunking, surf casting, and boat trolling spot.

Fishing starts in May with local trout, continues through the early chinook and coho salmon runs to "dog days" and time for harvest trout and jack salmon, continuing with fall salmon, and then winter steelhead which peak up in January and February. Flounder, perch, crabs, and clams are found in the bay all year 'round. The North Fork, especially, is a top fly fishing stream. Five Rivers is another good tributary.

A first rate, lovely river, which can support a major sport fishery, the Alsea today is much underrated.

The Alsea is best fished by boat from Drift Creek up. Numerous boat ramps, resorts, and boat rentals are located on the highway from Waldport up the south bank of the river.

Don Holm Photo

BILL YOUNG WITH A NICE STEELHEAD FROM THE SOUTH
FORK COQUILLE RIVER

Trip No. 30   Salmonberry River
                               Clatsop County
Alternates:
  Nehalem River
  Nehalem Bay

A rather remote and little-known river, the Salmon-berry heads up in the rugged, snaggy Tillamook Burn region north of the Wilson watershed and flows into the Nehalem below Elsie. It is accessible from Elsie via the river road.

A good sea-run cutthroat stream in the fall, a fair to good trout stream in the spring, it has a run of winter steelhead that peaks up in December and January. There is (or was) some top coho fishing near the junction with the Nehalem and is easily fished from the rocks. The salmon appear in October and November.

Don Holm Photo
ON THE OREGON COAST SALMON IS THE MOST IMPORTANT
PRODUCT

PART III

COLUMBIA RIVER

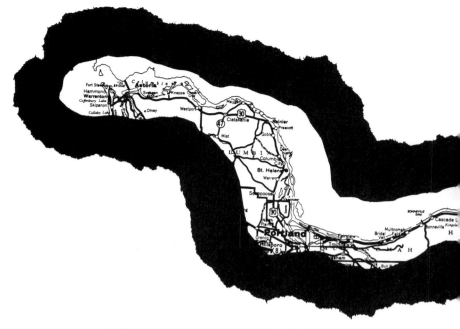

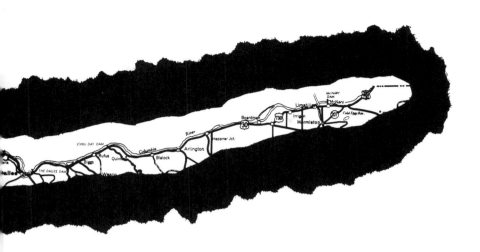

Photo Courtesy Oregon State Highway Travel Division

PUGET ISLAND ON THE LOWER COLUMBIA RIVER EAST OF
ASTORIA, OREGON

Trip No. 31   Columbia Estuary
Clatsop County

Alternates:
None

The lower Columbia from about Puget Island near Bradwood to the Bar is a brackish estuary about twenty-five miles long and in places nine miles wide. It is an awesome body of water, impossible to describe adequately, and one of the finest sport fisheries in the world.

Through this estuary come the frenzied runs of salmon, steelhead, smelt, cutthroat trout, and shad seeking spawning room. These upriver runs, scattered over the months from February to October, are met by young downstream migrants heading out to sea from as far away as the Continental Divide.

Within the estuary are permanent residents such as the white sturgeon (largest freshwater fish in North America), large populations of largemouth and small-

CHARTER BOAT FISHING OFF THE OREGON COAST

Don Holm Photo

mouth bass, crappies, catfish, bluegills, perch, to say nothing of native trouts.

Into the estuary from the sea also wander starry flounder, ocean perch, crabs, and other marine species. Under the mud of the flats are several varieties of clams.

Rich in history and colorful lumbering and fishing lore, the estuary is also a fascinating place to visit. Its many islands, sloughs, tributary rivers, bays, coves, and bayous would require half a lifetime to explore.

Lucky is the angler who has a boat suitable for these waters and the time to explore its byways leisurely. As yet the estuary on both sides of the river is sparsely settled and accessible only at a few places. It can be reached from U.S. 30 on the Oregon side in a number of places and on the Washington side from state highways.

Into the estuary flow Big Creek, Gnat Creek, Klaskanine, Youngs, Lewis and Clark, and Skipanon rivers on the Oregon side; Grays River, Naselle, and numerous creeks on the Washington side.

Services and accommodations are available at Astoria, Warrenton, Hammond, Knappa, Brownsmead, Bradwood, and scattered moorages and roadside shops.

There are relatively few boat launches and camping areas, and finding one's way around is difficult for a stranger. Recommended are a good highway map, local sportsmen's maps, and the U.S. Coast & Geodetic Survey chart for this section of the Columbia River.

When is the best time? Any time of the year. How? I'll still vote for a suitable boat that will go anywhere—even up into some of those obscure tidal creeks where you can find an occasional moss-covered ghost town left over from the old days.

Don Holm Photo

SHAD FISHING OFF WASHOUGAL RIVER

STURGEON FROM OFF TONGUE POINT, LOWER COLUMBIA

Don Holm Photo

Trip No. 32

Alternates:
  Anywhere in
  Vicinity

Lower Columbia
Multnomah County
Columbia County
Clatsop County

Incredible but true is the fact that much of the best angling available in the lower section of the West's great Columbia River goes almost unnoticed, because it happens to coincide with the fabulous offshore fishing. But for the contemplative angler who has a boat, a Coast & Geodetic navigation chart of the lower river, and an urge to explore, it is a paradise to be discovered.

You'll need heavy sturgeon gear, salmon and steelhead tackle, and a light spinning outfit. As a matter of fact, you might take a fly rod along, too. You're going to fish for the big prehistoric monsters, the white sturgeon (delicious smoked), sea-run cutthroat or "harvest trout," steelhead, native trout, shad, and even black bass, catfish, and crappies.

The sturgeon are in the deep holes from Bonneville to Tongue Point. They rise to bait of decayed fish, eels, or rotten meat. The sea-run cuts can be found in the main channel off the mouths of tributaries and along the islands and sandbars. The steelhead and salmon are in the main channels and off the mouths of tributaries. The panfish hang out in the backwater sloughs.

With literally hundreds of miles of fascinating and little-known waterways to explore along both sides of the lower Columbia, you have an all-year-around program cut out for you.

SMALLMOUTH BASS FROM THE MIDDLE COLUMBIA

BOAT HARBOR AT HAMMOND, OREGON

Trip No. 33   "Retirement Reach"
                         Multnomah County
Alternates:
    Willamette River
    Sandy River

I call the section of Columbia River from Sauvie Island to Bonneville Dam, "Retirement Reach." It is probably the most heavily fished stretch of river in the entire Northwest and offers the most variety. It flows through the Portland metropolitan area and is bordered on both sides by highways, freeways, and access roads. Detailed maps are necessary for the stranger, but there are more than two hundred moorages, boat launches, and sport shops on or adjacent to the good fishing "holes."

The popular beaches and bank plunking spots are easy to find, for they are occupied practically year 'round by an army of retired men and women who do little except fish. These spots include Walton and other beaches on the east side of Sauvie Island, Sun Dial Beach off the Sandy, and others in the vicinity of Tanner Creek below Bonneville.

The "hogline" holes for boat fishermen are too numerous to mention, but detailed sport maps usually give their locations.

Fishing is all-year-around for black bass, crappie, catfish, sturgeon and jack salmon. *Spring* is the time for shad, smelt, salmon, steelhead. *Summer* offers salmon, steelhead, and sea-run cutthroat (blueback, harvest trout, salmon trout). *Autumn* is the season for harvest trout, steelhead, chinook and coho salmon. *Winter* brings forth mostly steelhead.

Don Holm Photo

ART LACEY WITH A FAT SHAD FROM THE WILLAMETTE
RIVER AT THE FALLS

"SOCIAL SECURITY BEACH ON SAUVIE ISLAND"

Don Holm Photo

Trip No. 34

Alternates:
    Hood River
    Below Bonneville

Bonneville Pool
Hood River County
Wasco County

I first fished the Bonneville Pool section of the Columbia at Cascade Locks, where you could park within ten feet of the main salmon and steelhead channel. This is still possible, and the city of Cascade Locks now has a trailer park and other facilities there.

The impoundment behind Bonneville Dam is also accessible from numerous other points, such as Hood River, Mosier, Rowena, and Viento. There are several off-freeway parking areas where one can hike down to the water. And, since there are more boat launch sites than can be listed here, strangers should inquire locally.

DON HOLM WITH A COUPLE OF NICE WINTER STEELHEAD

Don Holm Photo

In addition to steelhead and salmon from mid-summer on, the angler has a choice of shad in early spring, as well as sea-run cutthroat in the fall ("harvest trout" or "bluebacks" or "salmon-trout"), native trout, whitefish, sturgeon, bass and panfish.

The water in this deepest part of the Gorge gets mighty rough at times, usually during afternoon winds. A good boat is a requirement, and so is some common sense.

Supplies and accommodations are located at communities along Interstate 80N on the Oregon side and U.S. 197 on the Washington side.

STEELHEAD FISHING ON THE COLUMBIA RIVER NEAR
ARLINGTON, OREGON

Photo Courtesy Oregon State Highway Travel Division

Trip No. 35

Alternates:
   Deschutes River
   John Day River

Celilo Lake
Wasco County
Sherman County

In the 1950s The Dalles Dam on the Columbia at the city of The Dalles drowned out the historic fishery at Celilo Falls, first described in detail by Lewis and Clark and mentioned by every traveler who came later. For a hundred years the Indian net fishery at the falls was a tourist attraction, and a mecca for sportsmen like myself for many years, too. Now it's all under water, and the lake it created continues to be a fine all year around sport fishing spot.

The shoreline sloughs and arms contain excellent bass and panfishing, including largemouths and smallmouths, and channel catfish. The deep underwater caverns created by the backwater have become havens for sturgeon. Salmon and steelhead are also caught from boats working over the deep channels.

The best spots for anadromous fishes are at or near the mouths of rivers and creeks. Off the Deschutes is probably the best known. There are a few selected places where bank plunking for salmon and steelhead can also be done; however, parking is limited along the freeway.

Local inquiry can be made at The Dalles, Biggs and Rufus. Supplies and accommodations are also available at these points. Boat launch sites are frequent and adequate.

Photo Courtesy Oregon State Highway Travel Division

THE COLUMBIA RIVER WEST OF THE DALLES, OREGON

Trip No. 36   Lake Umatilla
                Gilliam County
Alternates: *Morrow County*
    John Day River
    Deschutes River

Lake Umatilla is the impoundment behind the new John Day Dam on the Columbia, about twenty-eight miles upstream from The Dalles. It flooded out vast spawning areas for salmon and steelhead and forever eliminated the historic island duck and goose nesting areas. It is too soon to assess other adverse long-term effects.

The dam did create another huge inland sea, backing up water into dozens of semi-arid coulees and river and creek channels—many of them accessible by boat. It created also a paradise for the smallmouth, largemouth, crappie, catfish, and sturgeon fisherman. These can be fished all year 'round.

From late July on through the winter months, the lake should also be a fair to good place for salmon and steelhead, since the remaining runs have to swim through it. A few locals already have learned much about fishing these waters. In time some of these tricks will become better known.

The lake, of course, is reached via the water-level Interstate 80N freeway on the Oregon side and by State 14 on the Washington side.

Boaters should remember that this is an inland sea, and afternoon winds often create extremely hazardous conditions.

STURGEON FROM THE LOWER COLUMBIA

Trip No. 37   Lake Wallula
                               Umatilla County

Alternates:
  Walla Walla River
  Lake Umatilla

Oregonians still call Lake Wallula, the impoundment behind McNary Dam, the "McNary Pool," or even Mc-Nary Lake. This immense and virtually unused inland sea created when McNary Dam was built extends all the way up into Washington as far as the Tri-Cities. U.S. 730 and U.S. 395 skirt the water level through some fascinating geological formations on the Oregon side. Over on the Washington side, State roads and some county ruts give rare access.

There is a highway bridge at McNary Dam, with supplies and accommodations at Umatilla and Hermiston. Hat Rock State Park near the junction of U.S. 395 is a delightful off-highway park right on the shores of the lake, with boat landings, swimming area, and all facilities.

The lake has immense populations of smallmouth and largemouth bass, crappie, channel catfish, and sturgeon. It is so little fished, however, that only the locals know much about it. The backwaters and arms are best for the warmwater species.

There are steelhead and salmon to be had from late summer through winter, but they are hard to find. Deep trolling in the channel is most productive.

ROOSTER ROCK STATE PARK ON THE COLUMBIA RIVER, EAST OF PORTLAND, OREGON

PART IV

METROPOLITAN

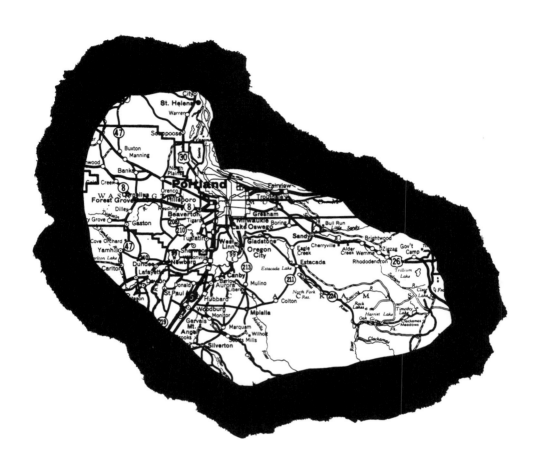

Trip No. 38   Lower Willamette
                               Multnomah County
Alternates:
    Clackamas River
    Columbia River

The stretch of the Willamette River below the Oregon City falls is the most important sport fishery within the boundaries of Oregon. It flows through the most densely populated metropolitan section of the state, and in recent years, with the federal government financing most of the cost, the Willamette salmon and steelhead runs have been rehabilitated as of old.

Some day—when the pollution problem is licked—this will be the finest steelhead and salmon water in all the Northwest. The upper Willamette watershed is, if given half a chance, a superb fish-spawning area, capable of sustaining tremendous runs.

Numerous moorages and boat launches are located along both sides of the Willamette. There are a number of popular hoglines for boaters—who, incidentally, must watch out for heavy commercial tug traffic! It is impossible for these craft to maneuver in the narrow channel.

Bank plunking is also possible at the falls, around the mouth of the Clackamas River, and various other minor spots from the falls to Multnomah Channel behind Sauvie Island.

All year fishing includes crappie, catfish, perch and bass in the shallows, sturgeon in the deep holes. Shad appear in June; steelhead and salmon fishing starts in February, continues to June. When there is a fall fishery again, it will start in September.

Photo Courtesy Oregon State Highway Travel Division

FISHING BOATS ON THE WILLAMETTE RIVER BELOW OREGON
CITY

Trip No. 39   Sauvie Island
                               Multnomah County
Alternates: *Columbia County*
   Columbia River
   Multnomah Channel

Historic Sauvie Island, largest in all Oregon, is located in the Columbia just below Linnton and is separated from the mainland by Multnomah Channel, a top salmon trolling spot. The island is about twenty miles long, and since the river runs nearly north and south at this point, the "east side" of the island where the bars and beaches are located is the "river" side.

The island contains several large lakes such as Sturgeon and McNary, and even a river called Gilbert River. All the lakes and streams on the island are affected by the ocean tides. In midsummer many of the lakes and sloughs dry up or nearly so, in winter they are in flood stage.

The lower end of the island is a game management area and no fishing is allowed during hunting season.

The principal species are bass and panfish, but during the salmon and steelhead season the beaches and bars are jammed with plunkers.

Because so many retired people fish from Walton, the public beach on the east side, it is more commonly known as "Social Security Beach." This has been a salmon and steelhead sport fishing spot for almost a hundred years.

Sauvie Island, incidentally, was named for a retired Hudson's Bay Company employee, was a Lewis and Clark campsite and in the early 1830s was the site of the first commercial salmon operation.

Trip No. 40   Timothy Lake
                               Clackamas County

Alternates:
    Clackamas River
    Trillium (Mud) Lake
    Washington County,
    Henry Hagg Lake

Timothy Lake is actually a nine hundred-acre impoundment on the upper Oak Grove Fork of the Clackamas River and can be reached via the new highway up the Clackamas from Estacada, or from Government Camp via the Skyline Road. It is well developed with picnic grounds and camping facilities and is heavily stocked with rainbows and cutthroat. It also has some brook trout. But in recent years, the kokanee (landlocked sockeye salmon) have filled the creels of fishermen.

Being so close to a metropolitan area, Timothy is heavily fished but is still a good spot for families. The campgrounds on the north shore can be reached only by boat. In most places, you can fish from the shore as well as a boat. Fly fishing is good in the late summer and fall.

Many other natural lakes in the vicinity can be reached by trails. A good forest service or quadrangle map is helpful in this area.

Photo Courtesy Oregon State Highway Travel Division

TIMOTHY LAKE AND A VIEW OF MOUNT HOOD

Trip No. 41   Clackamas River
                               Clackamas County
Alternates:
  Willamette River
  Sandy River
  Eagle Creek

When Rudyard Kipling visited Portland and fished the Clackamas River in the 1870s, he noted the adventure in his *American Travels* with the statement: "Ah! Now I have lived!" He was referring to salmon fishing with light tackle.

The Clackamas, which heads in the high Cascades near Olallie Lake and falls through rugged, deeply forested country (now badly logged off), was one of the finest fishing rivers in the world until logging, pollution and a series of blocking dams nearly ruined it. Today, mainly because of a massive federal hatchery on Eagle Creek, the salmon and steelhead runs are coming back— but nothing, of course, gets above the lowest of the concrete barriers. Everything above the dams is put-and-take fishing, strictly for tourists, kids and family outings.

The lower river, although subject to extreme fluctuations of the River Mill Dam, is a first rate winter steelhead stream now but hard to fish, since it is necessary to use a drift boat or jet sled. It has also a fair to good spring chinook run and a fall coho run.

Although adjacent to half the population of Oregon and subjected to fantastic pressure, the Clackamas River must still be classified as one of the best of its kind in the world.

Don Holm Photo

THE CLACKAMAS RIVER

Don Holm Photo

WINTER STEELHEAD FISHING
ON THE CLACKAMAS RIVER

CLACKAMAS RIVER
STEELHEAD FISHING

Don Holm Photo

Trip No. 42   Molalla River
                               Clackamas County
Alternates:
   Pudding River
   Clackamas River

The Molalla should be included in this compilation, because it is destined to be an important steelhead and possibly salmon river under the new rehabilitation programs. It is about fifty miles long, heading in the Cascades and flowing into the Willamette near Canby.

There is a lot of private land along it, and it gets low in midsummer; but once you get to know it, the Molalla is a productive stream, heavily stocked with rainbow and cuts and at present having a good winter steelhead run in late winter or early spring.

Its tributaries such as the North Fork, Trout Creek, Gribble Creek, Hancock, Milk, and others are good trout streams.

The town of Molalla is a good starting point. A stranger needs a road map and a large-scale topo map, or county map, as well. The upper sections of the river are accessible only by logging roads, some of which may not be open to the public.

AN EAGER ANGLER AT
HENRY-HAGG LAKE
ON OPENING DAY

Don Holm Photo

Trip No. 43   Pudding River
                               Clackamas County
Alternates:
  Willamette River
  Clackamas River

The first time I fished the Pudding, I was actually hunting wood ducks. My partner and I were floating it in a homemade canvas canoe, jump shooting. However, we noticed many fish rolling, so went back to the car for the fishing rods. When not hunting, we would do some casting, and this way picked up several good-sized smallmouth bass. The hunting was pretty good, too.

The Pudding heads in the foothills northeast of Salem, in Marion County, and flows through rolling farmland to join the Willamette near Canby in Clackamas County. The main stem is not stocked but many of its tributaries are, mostly with cutthroat and rainbow. Unknown by most anglers, however, some big trophy-type rainbows and steelhead are not infrequently dumped into the Pudding by hatchery personnel. These are spawned-out brood stock good for a couple more seasons when released in the wild.

The Pudding is also the recipient of the new federally financed salmon and steelhead rehabilitation programs on the Willamette system which includes the new ladders at the Oregon City falls. Someday it will be a major sport fishing stream and will help take the load from the metropolitan area.

Don Holm Photo

PUDDING RIVER

Don Holm Photo

SANDY RIVER

PART V

WILLAMETTE WATERSHED

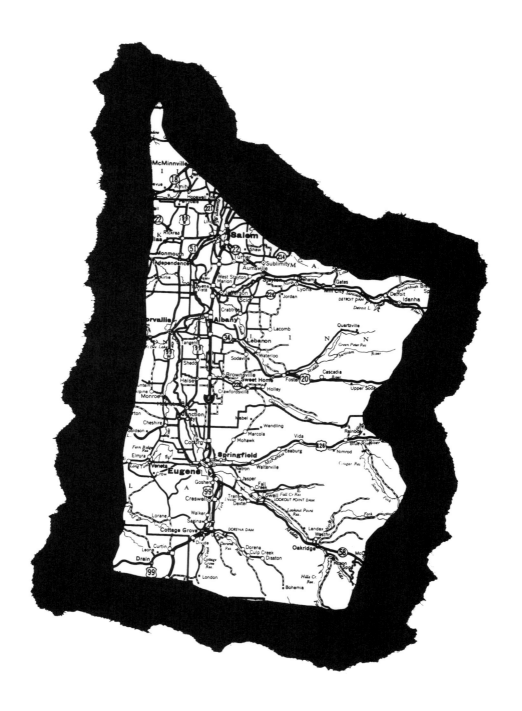

Trip No. 44

Alternates:
Tributaries

Mainstem Willamette
Clackamas County
Yamhill County
Polk County
Benton County
Linn County
Lane County

The historic Willamette River flows through some of the richest valley land in the world, as well as through two thirds of Oregon's population. Ever since the program called the "Willamette Greenway" was designed in response to public demand for pollution clean-up, there have been strong hopes that this river will become one of the nation's most important sport fishing streams.

Right now the middle section through the valley from Eugene to Oregon City falls is a vast, almost untouched, sport fishery that could stand a lot more pressure. The water gets rather low in the upper sections in midsummer, and the anadromous fish runs like salmon and steelhead tend to be scattered, but the resident trout and panfish fishing is worth anyone's attention.

The best, perhaps the only, way to fish this section of about one hundred miles is by boat. Cartoppers are okay and so are canoes—almost anything that will float. There are dozens of places to put in. An ideal vacation would be a week or two floating and fishing the meandering Willamette.

Fishing includes excellent cutthroat trout, channel catfish, largemouth and smallmouth bass, crappies, perch, bluegills, sturgeon, and even an occasional passing salmon or steelhead.

WILSONVILLE BRIDGE ON THE WILLAMETTE RIVER

Trip No. 45   Waldo Lake
                         Lane County
Alternates:
    Odell Lake
    Crane Prairie
    Hills Creek

The second largest lake in Oregon, located on the ridge of the Cascades, can now be reached by car on a paved road. Waldo Lake drains into the Willamette and is reached via State 58 to Willamette Pass, then north on a new road up through the forest; or from Cultus Lake over a network of forest roads on the east slope. From June on the road is passable, but often has snow.

There are campgrounds and trailer sites—and recently, boat launchings. A lot of pressure is expected to be put on this once-pristine wilderness. The lake has been heavily stocked with rainbow, brook trout, and kokanee.

The water is deep, clear, and cold but fish food is marginal. Some trout going to five pounds are known to be in the lake.

This is a large lake subject to high winds and sudden afternoon storms, which means that anglers should bring good boats and use common sense. Best fishing spots will be in the shoal areas, except during the hottest part of the summer.

A beautiful spot, a rare sort of lake, and fair to good fishing prospects for the future. Expect a lot of company.

Trip No. 46   The Santiams
                                Linn County
Alternates: *Marion County*
    Detroit Lake
    Breitenbush

The Santiams—North and South and Little North Santiam—drain a large section of the Cascades, come together near Albany and flow into the Willamette near Buena Vista. These rivers are ice cold, dangerous to wade, swim or boat, and they plunge through some rugged, forested real estate. The fishing is fair to good.

The North Santiam has the honor of being blocked by Detroit Dam, which also is a steady trout producer. The Little North Santiam heads in Elk Lake and is a good trout and steelhead producer. The Breitenbush River is also a major tributary, flowing into the Detroit Reservoir. South Santiam furnished the excuse to build Green Peter Dam to say nothing of Foster, which now also provide some slackwater pond fishing.

Photo Courtesy Oregon State Highway Travel Division

DETROIT LAKE

NORTH SANTIAM
RIVER EAST OF
SALEM, OREGON

Photo Courtesy Oregon State Highway Travel Division

U.S. 20 from Albany and Lebanon goes up the South Santiam, and State 22 from Salem goes to the North drainage. These highways also run across the Cascades to the Deschutes system and the hundreds of mountain lakes. Traffic on these highways is usually heavy during the season. There are numerous campgrounds, especially around Detroit; and in the national forest areas, hundreds of miles of logging and secondary roads.

The lower Santiams are rapidly becoming prime winter steelhead and spring salmon waters.

Trip No. 47   McKenzie River
                               Lane County
Alternates:
   South Fork
   Cougar Reservoir
   Calapooia

It would be a shame to pass up the famous McKenzie River, home of the McKenzie Redsides and former haunt of such famous anglers as Herbert Hoover and Zane Grey. Although not the river it used to be, it is still above average.

The McKenzie heads in the Cascades in the Three Sisters Wilderness Area and is accessible via U.S. 126 from Eugene or Sisters. McKenzie Pass, however, is not open in winter.

There is much private land along the stream, but many places can be found for plunking. The ideal way to fish it, of course, is with a McKenzie drift boat and a guide, and many people do. The fly fishing is very good at times and good most of the season.

The river is stocked with hatchery rainbows, and there are also cutthroat and whitefish in the river.

A run of chinook salmon in the spring is getting better each year. Check the *Synopsis* for local angling regulars, as there are many exceptions.

The area is heavily fished and has lots of traffic during the season. Campgrounds are available and numerous roadside establishments can be found.

Don Holm Photo

WALDO LAKE

Photo Courtesy Oregon State Highway Travel Division

FISHERMEN ON THE McKENZIE
RIVER

Photo Courtesy Oregon State Highway Travel Division

TROUT FISHING ON THE
McKENZIE RIVER AT NIMROD

Trip No. 48   Pamelia Lake
                           Linn County

Alternates:
    Detroit Lake
    Breitenbush River

An old favorite with Oregonians, particularly those from Salem and Eugene, is Pamelia. Located, like Olallie, almost on the summit of the Cascades, it can be reached up the Pamela Creek Road which takes off about thirteen miles above Detroit from the Santiam highway, State 22. At this writing, the road stops about two miles from the lake, but it's an easy hike in.

Pamelia is top cutthroat water and also has some nice brook trout. Because the fish grow too fast for the available food supply, anglers are allowed to catch thirty fish a day, and the season is open all year. A rubber raft is handy at Pamelia. Fly fishing is good early and late. There are also a number of small lakes within hiking distance.

A lot of anglers wait each spring for the chance to be the first one into Pamelia. Most years they begin trying in late May or early June. The nights are still cold then and the snow drifts remain in abundance—but that's all part of the fun and the challenge.

Trip No. 49   Middle Fork Willamette
                               Lane County

Alternates:
  Hills Creek
  Odell Lake
  Crescent Lake

Middle Fork, major tributary of the Willamette, heads in the Cascades near Cowhorn Mountain south of Crescent and is joined by Hills Creek, Fall Creek, and the Coast Fork to become the main Willamette River. The dam builders have conquered most of these with the new Hills Creek Dam, Lookout Point, Dorena—all of which now sport reservoirs—to say nothing of the Fern Ridge Reservoir on the Long Tom Fork on the other side of the valley.

The Middle Fork, Lookout Point, Hills Creek are all accessible up the State highway 58 from Springfield, which connects with U.S. 97 near Chemult. Much of the river is within Willamette Forest and this is honeycombed with logging roads and Jeep trails. The secondary road up the upper Middle Fork was in good condition the last time I traveled that route and continued over the hump on a dirt track to Crescent Lake through Emigrant Pass and around the Diamond Peak Wild Area.

The Middle Fork is heavily stocked—almost entirely with rainbow and cutthroat.

The North Fork Willamette, the stream which drains Waldo Lake, is better fishing; however, conditions can change quickly.

Photo Courtesy Oregon State Highway Travel Division

UPPER NORTH FALLS, IN SILVER FALLS STATE PARK

PART VI

SOUTHERN OREGON

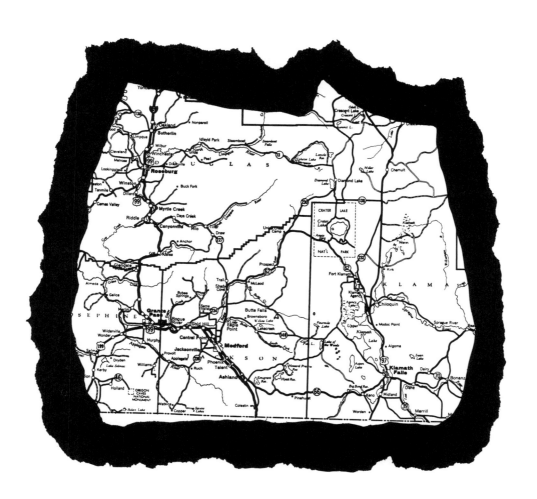

Trip No. 50   Lake of the Woods
                                Klamath County
Alternates:
  None

Ice fishing is a popular and common winter sport in the northern tier of states—and virtually an "industry" in places like Minnesota and Wisconsin. Until recently, however, it has been almost unknown in the Pacific Northwest, except in the Pothole Lakes of Northeastern Washington. In the 1960s many Western states began opening selected high lakes to winter ice fishing. The first of these was Oregon's Lake of the Woods 5,000 feet up in the southern Cascades.

In the Winema National Forest, this popular summer vacation mecca withstands heavy pressure, especially from Californians. The lake contains brook and rainbow trout and kokanees (landlocked sockeye salmon). The original purpose of opening the lake for ice fishing was to reduce the brookie population.

Once inaccessible by auto, Lake of the Woods can now be reached by State 140 highway from Medford or Klamath Falls. January is the best fishing month. There are no tourist accommodations during the winter, so bring your own camper or plan to return to town. As in all mountain country in winter, *go prepared.*

For gear a short boat rod, jig pole, or handline is suitable. You'll also need an ice auger to make a hole, of course. Jig flies, worms, small lures, salmon eggs, crawdad tails—anything used to fish with during the summertime—will work through the ice.

Photo Courtesy Oregon State Highway Travel Division

LAKE OF THE WOODS IN KLAMATH COUNTY, WITH MOUNT
McLOUGHLIN IN THE BACKGROUND

Trip No. 51   Upper Rogue

Josephine County

Alternates: *Jackson County*

    Diamond Lake   *Douglas County*

    Klamath Lake

From below Grants Pass on upstream past the Gold Ray Dam, through Gold Hill, Shady Cove, Trail, and to the headwaters in the mountains is the heavily fished Upper Rogue. There are good roads and easy access along most of this section. Be sure to check the regulations carefully, as there are numerous closures and exceptions. Numerous campgrounds, state parks, picnic areas, and resorts around this popular tourist mecca get rather overrun in the summer time.

During the heat of the summer, the water in the river gets low, warm, and often polluted with municipal and domestic wastes and agricultural residues. I have measured the temperature of the river below Grants Pass at almost 80 degrees.

The Upper Rogue is a heavily planted trout stream, and in recent years rehabilitation efforts by the Game Commission have resulted in some healthy runs of summer steelhead, chinook salmon, and winter steelhead. Visitors unfamiliar with the river should hire a guide and boatman—especially during the salmon and steelhead season. It's cheaper and more satisfying in the long run. That is, if you want to catch fish.

FISHING ON THE ROGUE RIVER ABOVE TRAIL

Trip No. 52

Alternates:
  Illinois River

Middle Rogue
Curry County
Josephine County

You don't want to miss the "Wild River" wilderness of the Middle Rogue. If you have four days or so, hire a boat and guide at Grants Pass and make the trip down to Gold Beach. If you only have a day or so, take one of the whitewater jet boats up from Wedderburn to the Paradise Bar lodge.

On the four- or five-day trip you'll camp out on the bars and beaches, meander along, fishing the virgin holes, and enjoy one of the finest wilderness areas left. In summer you'll have lots of company on this popular excursion as the river becomes a freeway of boats and rafts. You'll stop at such historic spots as Galice, Marial, Black Bar, Hellgate, Grave Creek, Paradise Bar, Winkle Bar (Zane Grey's old lodge), Illahe, and Agness. The trip costs approximately $200 a person and is worth every bit of it.

Advance reservations are necessary, and contact can be made through Grants Pass Chamber of Commerce or the Oregon Guides and Packers Association.

RAPIDS OF THE ROGUE RIVER

BETWEEN STRETCHES OF "WHITE WATER" ON THE ROGUE
RIVER

Trip No. 53

Alternates:
Rogue River
Illinois River

Applegate River
Josephine County
Jackson County

The Applegate River starts on Mt. Ashland and flows through a narrow valley west of the divide near Jacksonville, down through farming communities to join the Rogue below Grants Pass. It's named after the Applegate party of pioneers who came into Oregon via the southern route after much hardship.

The river gets low in the summer and is considered a fragile fishing stream with limited access. You can reach it via a streamside secondary road from Grants Pass or Jacksonville, the historic old mining town. There is a short steelhead season in December, and another in January and February. No salmon fishing is permitted. The regulations are confusing, so check the *Synopsis* carefully.

The stream is well stocked with trout and fishing for it is best in the spring months. Angling from boats is not allowed. Be sure to get permission before entering private land. There is a campground and picnic area at the bridge crossing halfway up.

Photo Courtesy Oregon State Highway Travel Division

HELLGATE CANYON ON THE LOWER ROGUE RIVER

Trip No. 54   Illinois River
                             Curry County
Alternates: *Josephine County*
    Rogue River
    Applegate River

The lower Illinois, which enters the Rogue near Agness, heads in the old gold mining districts across the border in California and flows through the sunny valleys of southern Oregon in the Grants Pass area, then plunges through some of the wildest mountains in the West. The upper sections are accessible by road, but from the mouth up through the lower gorge, it's all trail work and very few people take the time or effort to enjoy it.

It is a superb steelhead river, as well as a good chinook and coho stream in the late fall. Most of the fish are taken from boats in the Kerby area or those coming up into the river from the Rogue.

Check regulations. From the mouth to Pomeroy Dam the river is open for salmon all year. Winter regulations permit trout not less than twelve inches in length. (Steelhead and cutthroat are regarded as trout.) The river is closed to all angling from Fall Creek to four hundred feet above Illinois Falls.

Supplies and accommodations are available at Gold Beach, Grants Pass, Selma and other points.

Take a gold pan along and dig around some of the sandbars. You might become independently wealthy.

Don Holm Photo

FLOATING THE FAMOUS ROGUE

Photo Courtesy Oregon State Highway Travel Division

LAKE SELMAC, WEST OF SELMA

Trip No. 55   North Umpqua
                           Douglas County
Alternates:
    South Umpqua
    Diamond Lake
    Lemolo Lake

The North Umpqua is another Oregon stream which has attracted famous anglers like Zane Grey and Herbert Hoover. The North river flows into the main Umpqua below Roseburg, but most of its course is in the Umpqua National Forest and its source is in Diamond Lake. A smaller "lake" (actually a power company reservoir), Lemolo, is a delightful and charming spot with a surprisingly good brown trout fishery.

The principal tributaries are Steamboat Creek, Rock Creek, Little River.

The North Umpqua is subject to special regulations, so check the *Synopsis*. Spring salmon fishing is permitted below the deadline at Rock Creek from January 1 through June 12; below the Mott Bridge, jack salmon can be taken all year with a five-fish limit. The steelhead season above the Mott deadline is May 24 through September 1; the "large trout" (over twelve inches) are legal November 1 through May 23 below Mott deadline; the eight-inch trout limit is in effect from May 24 through September 1 below the Mott Bridge; and the six-inch trout limit is in effect from April 29 through October 31 in the North Umpqua and tributaries above Soda Springs Dam.

The North Umpqua is a superb flyfishing stream, and the steelhead program has brought the river back to its former greatness.

Photo Courtesy Oregon State Highway Travel Division

LEMOLO FALLS, LOCATED ALONG THE NORTH UMPQUA RIVER
IN EASTERN DOUGLAS COUNTY

Trip No. 56   South Umpqua
                               Douglas County
Alternates:
    North Umpqua
    Diamond Lake

The South Umpqua has its head in Fish Lake in the Cascades near Crater Lake and flows down through the Umpqua National Forest to Canyonville, Myrtle Creek, and Roseburg. Interstate freeway 5 follows the lower section of it, and State 227 and the network of forest roads supply access to most of the upper reaches.

This is a salmon and steelhead river, with the rehabilitated steelhead runs in recent years going almost unnoticed except by local people. They are a result of modern fish management programs.

The water gets low in midsummer but is heavily stocked, and the spring and fall trout fishing is good. The Umpqua system has its own special angling regulations so check the *Synopsis* closely. One should not overlook the tributaries such as Elk Creek, Cow Creek, Jackson Creek, and Days Creek, which are all good trout fishing.

The upper section, being in national forest areas, has numerous campgrounds, but much of the lower run is bordered by private land or otherwise inaccessible—to say nothing of being subject to pollution from municipalities and mills.

Don Holm Photo

DIAMOND LAKE

Trip No. 57   Williamson River
                               Klamath County

Alternates:
    Sprague River
    Agency Lake
    Wood River

The Williamson, which flows into the north end of Upper Klamath Lake, heads in the Klamath Marsh area of the Winema National Forest to the northeast. This was once one of the world's most famous rivers, with rainbow trout going to fifteen and twenty pounds or better, but in recent years it has declined some. It is heavily fished, and a lot of people are attracted by the spring mullet season when snagging is allowed and a carnival atmosphere prevails.

While the river is reached via U.S. 97 to Chiloquin, north of Klamath Falls, and logging roads give access to many parts, much of the river is bordered by private land —and fishing from boats is illegal. The fly fishing is excellent when and where you can get it, and in addition to big rainbows there are some nice brook and brown trout in the river. The standard spinning lures work well, either trolled or drift cast.

The river usually opens with the high lakes season in late May. Anglers will find facilities, accommodations, boat ramps, and other necessities in the vicinity of the highway bridge.

Trip No. 58   Klamath Lake
                               Klamath County

Alternates:
    Agency Lake
    Fourmile Lake
    Lake of the Woods
    Fish Lake

Oregon's largest lake, more than thirty miles long
and ten miles wide, Klamath contains a number of species
of fish including rainbows, a sort of freshwater mullet,
bass and panfish, and miscellaneous scrap fish. The
lake is quite shallow, which prevents it from being an
outstanding fishing spot, but some of the rainbow get to
be truly big whoppers—up to twenty pounds.

The best fishing is in the north end of the lake around
Pelican Bay and in Agency Lake. Best method is by
trolling large lures.

U.S 97 highway runs along the east side of the lake,
and State 140 gives access to the west side as well as to
the Cascade lakes in the Rogue River National Forest.

Klamath Falls at the lower end of the lake is the nearest city, but there are many facilities in the surrounding
national forests for campers and anglers.

Trip No. 59   Klamath River
                           Klamath County
Alternates:
    Klamath Lake
    Howard Prairie
    Agency Lake

The famous Klamath River heads in upper Klamath Lake, Oregon's largest natural freshwater lake, which is fed by drainage from the high Cascades around Crater Lake. But only about sixty miles of the river flows through Oregon. It enters California near Grizzly Mountain, and then winds a tortuous way through the Siskiyous for two hundred miles to the Pacific Ocean.

The California section is a major salmon and steelhead river and is heavily fished, almost to the point of being ludicrous to watch. If you have ever seen the hoglines at the mouth during the salmon season you'll know what I mean. But the fame of "California's" Klamath River is worldwide, and not without some reason—chinooks go to thirty-five pounds and steelhead to eighteen. It also has the famous summer run of "half-pounders" which weigh in about four to five pounds.

The river is followed by a road along most of its length in California. In Oregon State 66 follows it for about thirty miles, and from there to Beswick there is an unimproved road along the bank. The Oregon section, above the Copco Dam, is mostly for planted rainbows, bass, and panfish.

Trip No. 60   Odell Lake
                               Klamath County

Alternates:
  Crescent Lake
  Crescent Creek
  Little Deschutes
  Davis Lake

Odell Lake cannot be passed up, not only because it is large but also because it is one of the best fishing lakes, even with the heavy pressure it gets. Its neighbor, Crescent, is also a top fishing spot.

Odell lies along State Highway 58 near Willamette Pass on the east slope and is about five or six miles long. It is very deep and has a large population of lake trout or mackinaw, as well as lots of large kokanee. There are also rainbow, dolly varden, and whitefish in the lake. Some of the lake trout reach around thirty pounds, and the kokanee seem to grow large, too.

The lake is subject to high winds in the afternoon. The mosquitoes are abundant in the spring and early summer, but the wind blows them away. There are resorts there, with cabins and boat rentals, and several campgrounds in the vicinity. There is also an airstrip close by.

MACKINAW TROUT FROM ODELL LAKE

ODELL LAKE IN THE CASCADE MOUNTAIN RANGE

PART VII

DESCHUTES BELT

Don Holm Photo

FISHING MEANS GOOD EATIN'

Don Holm Photo

Don Holm Photo

ONG THE MIDDLE DESCHUTES

Trip No. 61   Middle Deschutes
                               Deschutes County

Alternates:
    Metolius River
    Crooked River
    Warm Springs River

Until a private utility built two concrete barriers in the middle section, the Deschutes River was considered one of the finest trout and salmon streams in the world, flowing through one of the more awesome canyons on this continent and filled with the purest of mountain spring water. It is still a formidable sport fishing stream, in spite of the two inland lakes behind the dams—Lake Simtustus and Lake Billy Chinook. As a matter of fact, these impoundments have tended to lower the water temperature in the lower river and thus have had some beneficial effect on fish, even though the dams do block the passage of anadromous species.

There is limited access to the river, down into the canyon from the rim on a few Jeep roads, and along the river banks from several access points by dirt road, but most of the river is locked up by private ownership or sheer inaccessibility. Two popular access points are Maupin, a little oasis on State 216, and South Junction reached from U.S. 97 on an adventure road.

Most effective is a float trip from White Horse Rapids to Maupin, or a trip on a jet sled with a competent guide. It is much too hot down in the canyon during July and August, but a few people do attempt it. At other times it is a superb fishing experience, which will reward one with brown trout, whitefish, planted rainbows, and the famed "redsides," or native rainbow.

For spin fishing, use the small "roostertail" lures or

weighted wobblers. In season use hellgrammites and salmon flies (May). For fly casters, a tied-down caddis is hard to beat, or any May fly imitation.

Fish the fast water, not the pools, especially during hot weather, for this is where the fish seek oxygen. And the rattlesnake danger is real at all times, especially in weeds and brush along the shore.

Photo Courtesy Oregon State Highway Travel Division

FINE CATCH FROM THE DESCHUTES
RIVER NEAR BEND, OREGON

Photo Courtesy Oregon State Highway Travel Division

THE UPPER DESCHUTES SOUTHWEST
OF BEND, OREGON, IN THE PRINGLE
FALLS AREA

Trip No. 62   Lower Deschutes River
                                    Deschutes County
Alternates:
  John Day River
  Klickitat River
  Main Stem Columbia

Even in the late 1940s when Governor Morrie Griswold of Nevada landed the world record summer steelhead on a Norwegian Moustache, the mouth of the Deschutes River and its lower reaches was a popular mecca for the dedicated angler. Prominent fly fishermen came from all over the United States to fish it. Since then a private utility company has dammed the upper section of this superb river with two barriers to anadromous fishes, and the Corps of Engineers placed another huge barrier on the main Columbia, flooding out historic Celilo Falls and backing water up to the Deschutes canyon.

The famed Deschutes summer run of steelhead, however, seems to be holding its own, and today where one angler used to beat the water there are ten competing for the same spot. Beginning traditionally on July 4, this fine run of fish appears in the Deschutes. Because much of the lower river is inaccessible except on foot, by jet sled, or by railroad, the run is maintaining itself in spite of the pressure.

For summer steelhead you need a suitable spinning outfit, with six to ten-pound-test line and weighted wobblers in the half-ounce to three-quarter-ounce class. You "drift" the lure through a run of fast water, hitting the tail-out at the bottom of the swing, and bouncing the lure along the bottom. This means a lot of hang-ups, but it's the only way to reach the fish.

Fly fishing is done essentially the same way in such

water, using a sink tip or weighted line and streamer flies. The ironheads don't hit hard, so you must raise the rod at the slightest bump or you'll miss the strike.

Fishing from a boat or raft, incidentally, is forbidden on the Deschutes.

Finally, this is rattlesnake country, and don't ever forget it!

The lower 100 miles of the Deschutes is now in wild and scenic river status. It is also on the state's special "wild fish" enhancement list, which includes reduced bag limits, artificial lures, and catch-and-release for steelhead. Check the latest *Synopsis of Angling Regulations* carefully.

THE DESCHUTES RIVER IN THE LOWER BRIDGE AREA NEAR REDMOND IN CENTRAL OREGON

Photo Courtesy Oregon State Highway Travel Division

Trip No. 63   Warm Springs
                                    Reservation
Alternates: *Wasco County*
    Deschutes River   *Jefferson County*

The Warm Springs Indian Reservation in Central Oregon contains some of the prettiest country in Oregon and some of the best fishing. Covering an area as large as many eastern states, the reservation extends from the Deschutes River west to the summit of the Cascades.

Administered by the Tribal Council of the Confederated Tribes of the Warm Springs Reservation, a very progressive management organization, the lakes and streams on the reservation are open to the public on a permit basis. Permits (in addition to the regular Oregon fishing license) can be obtained for a nominal fee from the tribal headquarters at Warm Springs or from numerous sporting goods stores around the state.

The tribe has an effective conservation department, and regulations are enforced.

Some of the best fishing is in the Warm Springs River, the Cascades lakes, the west shore of the Deschutes River, the west side of Lake Simtustus behind Pelton Dam, the west side of Lake Billy Chinook behind Round Butte Dam, and the Metolius River.

One of the finest luxury resorts in the West, incidentally, is the Kah-Nee-Ta hot springs resort north of the agency headquarters.

Trip No. 64

Crane Prairie and
Wickiup
Deschutes County

Alternates:
Deschutes River
Davis Lake
Cultus Lake

The famous twin lakes, Crane Prairie and Wickiup, are really dammed up reservoirs in the main channel of the Deschutes River and are located off Century Drive southwest of Bend. They are virtually surrounded by half a hundred small and large lakes in this east slope Cascades lake country.

In the past some record brown and rainbow trout have come from these waters but in recent years they have tapered off—a characteristic of most reservoirs. Crane Prairie boasts not only rainbow and brown trout, but kokanees, brook trout, and even landlocked coho salmon. Lately these waters have been plagued by scrap fish so at present the future is clouded.

Wickiup is a large impoundment and has been a top scorer in the state for giant rainbow and brown trout, kokanees, and coho salmon. It is a good fly fishing lake—in fact, all methods of fishing produce here.

Campgrounds, resorts, boat rentals, and other facilities are available in the area.

There are some local closures, so check the *Synopsis*.

Photo Courtesy Oregon State Highway Travel Division

CRANE PRAIRIE RESERVOIR IN THE OREGON CASCADE MOUNTAINS

Trip No. 65   East and Paulina Lakes
                               Deschutes County

Alternates:
    Deschutes River
    Paulina Creek

Two of the Oregon lakes best known to outsiders, especially Californians, are East and Paulina, lovely bodies of water high up in the Newberry Crater southeast of Bend. They are reached via U.S. 97 south to the junction, then by secondary road up to the crater. It's worth the trip just to see these lakes.

East has mostly rainbows, with some brookies and brown trout. Rainbows have measured five pounds, browns ten, but this is unusual. Currently the fishing is rather disappointing compared to the old days, but conditions do change—both ways.

Paulina, the twin, contains rainbow, brook, and occasionally brown trout. Some of the fish get quite large, but the average is around twelve inches.

During the hot summer, the fish head for the deep water. Best fishing is early and late in the season.

These lakes open with the high lakes season at the end of May but because of snow may not be accessible that early. They are in the 6,000- to 7,000-foot-elevation zones, and nights are cold even in the summer. There are many resorts and campgrounds, and complete facilities are available.

Photo Courtesy Oregon State Highway Travel Division

PAULINA LAKE, SOUTHEAST OF BEND, OREGON

Don Holm Photo

BROWN TROUT FROM
EAST LAKE

Trip No. 66   Prineville Reservoir
                               Crook County

Alternates:
   Ochoco Reservoir
   Crooked River
   Antelope Flat

An excellent artificial lake about fifteen miles long
has been formed by a dam on the Crooked River above
Prineville. This is hot, dry, rimrock country, complete
with rattlesnakes, but Prineville Reservoir forms a nice
oasis. It can be reached via three secondary roads from
the city of Prineville.

There is a resort, with boat rentals, and supplies at
the lake, a county and state park, and plenty of places to
fish even from the shore.

The bass fishing at this writing is the best in this
part of the state. Catfishing is good at night, and the
rainbow trout fishing is fair to good. There is some good
fly fishing here late in the evening much of the summer.

Trip No. 67   Olallie Lake
                         Jefferson County

Alternates:
   Breitenbush Lake
   Timothy Lake

A beautiful mountain jewel nestled on the summit of the Cascades, beneath Mt. Jefferson, Olallie Lake is an idyllic paradise that has been a favorite with anglers— especially fly fishermen—for seventy-five years. Today you can drive right to it on good roads, although the last few miles are gravel. One route is up the Clackamas River highway—follow the signs. Another route is on the Skyline Road from U.S. 26 near Government Camp. A third is up the Breitenbush River from Detroit. In the old days you hiked in or rode horseback.

Olallie is now heavily planted, but its clear sweet water raises some nice rainbow, cutthroat, and brook trout. No motors are allowed, but there is no nicer way to spend a day or two than by drifting around its shoreline, fly casting.

There are resort and boat rentals, several forest service campgrounds, and lots of mosquitoes until late summer and fall.

Olallie, incidentally, drains down the east side of the Cascades and at least fifty other good, but small, lakes are within hiking distance.

Photo Courtesy Oregon State Highway Travel Division

OLALLIE LAKE IN THE NORTHERN OREGON CASCADES

Trip No. 68   Fall River
                               Deschutes County

Alternates:
    Crane Prairie
    Deschutes River
    Wickiup

A very fine but little known fly-fishing-only stream in the famous Deschutes Belt, Fall River is often passed by in favor of Wickiup and Crane Prairie. It is only about eleven miles long, flowing into the Deschutes in the vicinity of Pringle Falls. It is accessible by forest roads and easily waded. Private land borders it in some places.

The river is heavily stocked with legals and also contains some native rainbow and brown trout as well as brooks. It is clear, cold, spring fed and pretty. The fishing is good all season.

Mosquitoes are abundant in spring and early summer. Campgrounds are numerous in the area.

FALL RIVER IN CENTRAL OREGON
Photo Courtesy Oregon State Highway Travel Division

Trip No. 69   Hosmer Lake
                                Deschutes County

Alternates:
  Todd Lake
  Sparks Lake
  Little Lava Lake
  Lava Lake
  Elk Lake

Hosmer Lake, an obscure body of water in the country southwest of Bend, formerly called Mud Lake, is included mainly because it contains Oregon's experiment in raising Atlantic salmon. It is about 160 acres in size and has, besides the salmon, some brook and rainbow trout.

Hosmer is one of the few places in the country where an Atlantic salmon can be caught—but with barbless hooks and they must be thrown back.

Dedicated fly fishermen really have a time when they are hitting. They are leapers, running to about eighteen inches maximum. Standard wet fly patterns take them, but because these fish are extremely wary, a little more skill is necessary with dry flies.

A lot of anglers will think this is a lot of fuss over fish you can't even keep long enough to photograph, but then it all depends on what your reasons are for going fishing in the first place.

You can reach Hosmer and the other lakes via Century Drive, the loop highway from Bend.

METOLIUS RIVER
WITH VIEW OF
MOUNT JEFFERSON
IN BACKGROUND

THREE CREEKS
LAKE, LOCATED
SOUTH OF SISTERS,
OREGON

BLUE LAKE, LOCATED
A HALF MILE WEST
OF SUTTLE LAKE

Trip No. 70   Metolius River
                                Jefferson County

Alternates:
  Blue Lake
  Suttle Lake
  Three Creeks

The Metolius is Oregon's classic dry fly fishing stream, located in a beautiful park-like ponderosa pine setting just down on the east slope of the Cascades from the summit, under the lee of Three Fingered Jack and Black Butte. Its head is in the springs near Camp Sherman, and it flows into the Deschutes and what is now the Metolius Arm of Lake Billy Chinook, otherwise called Round Butte Reservoir. The Metolius runs along the southern boundary of Warm Springs Indian Reservation, a clear, rapid, cold, sparkling stream which changes little winter or summer and is now heavily stocked. Fishing is prohibited above the Camp Sherman bridge, and fly fishing only is permitted below there for ten miles.

The Wizard Falls fish hatchery is about five miles downstream from Camp Sherman. Guides, supplies, and cabins are available. There are a number of campgrounds along the road that follows the river about twenty miles downstream and continues on as a trail on the south, or public lands, side. The stream has some big dolly varden and fairly good rainbow trout.

Nowhere is there a more picturesque and classic fly-fishing stream and anyone who uses bait or hardware here is definitely an outcast.

PART VIII

NORTHEAST OREGON

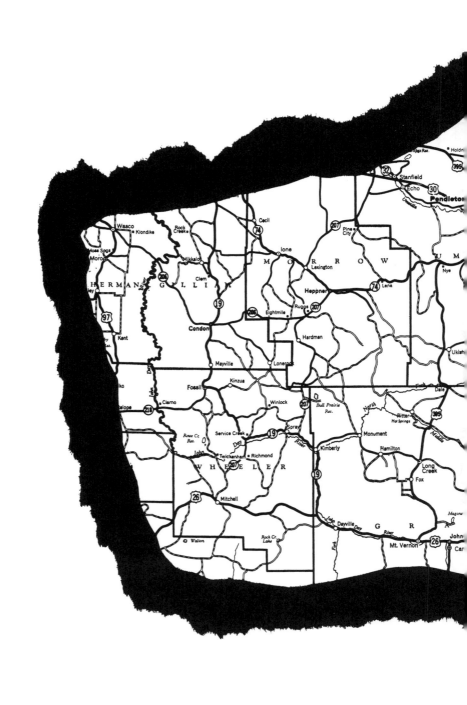

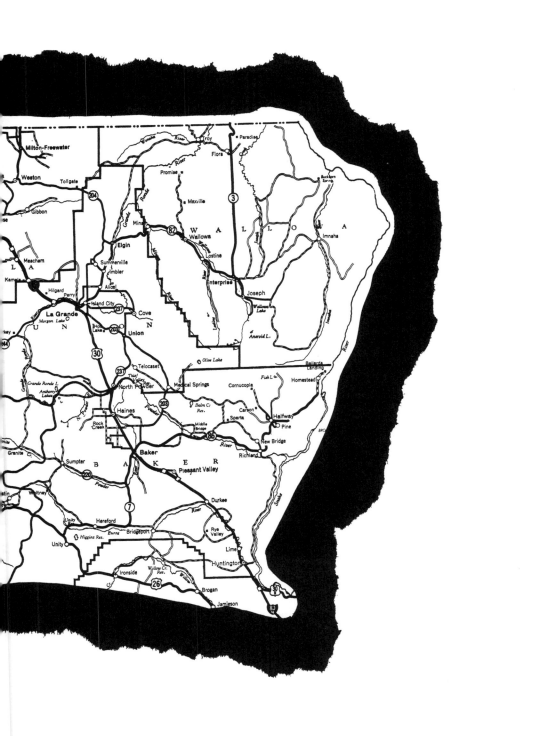

Trip No. 71   Umatilla River (lower)
                               Umatilla County

Alternates:
  Columbia River
  Walla Walla River

Flowing through semi-arid, irrigated cattle and wheat country, the Umatilla enters the Columbia just below McNary Dam. It becomes so low during the dry season that the lower section is merely a series of pools, but like many such rivers in Oregon the young steelhead fry survive in these pools until the first rains flush them out and send them off to sea.

The lower Umatilla is a good steelhead stream from November until April and is a fairly good winter salmon river as well. It is closed to all angling for three hundred feet below and two hundred feet above the Threemile Dam, the Westland Dam and the Cold Springs Dam. All diversions and canals are also closed. Below the three hundred-foot limit at Threemile Dam, however, is one of the best steelhead spots. The months of December, January, February, and March are best.

Secondary roads follow the Umatilla through most of its length below Pendleton. Much of it is private land, but access is available at road crossings and railroad grades. At times it is also possible to drift the river.

Photo Courtesy Oregon State Highway Travel Division

THE UMATILLA RIVER NEAR BAR-M RANCH

Trip No. 72   John Day Arm
                               Gilliam County
Alternates: *Sherman County*
  Willow Creek Arm
  Columbia River

The pool formed by construction of the John Day Dam on the Columbia River, sometimes called "Lake Umatilla," is a huge new inland sea with a great future recreational potential. Among the best features of this impoundment are the remote, fascinating, and almost inaccessible arms of the lake where the water has backed up into canyons and coulees. One of these, the John Day Arm, where the water has backed up into the John Day River canyon for nine or ten miles, now contains some of the finest smallmouth bass fishing in the country—and is almost totally untouched.

You can launch a boat from a new facility at the mouth of the John Day, below Interstate 80N (the John Day canyon is inaccessible except by foot or boat), and fish up into the canyon as far as The Narrows, about ten miles above the mouth. The water depth varies from fifty feet or so below The Narrows to well over a hundred feet at the mouth.

Halfway up the Arm there is a superb marine park with complete facilities but accessible only by boat.

Fish anywhere and expect not only smallmouths but crappie, sturgeon, whitefish, trout, steelhead, or salmon.

A NICE CRAPPIE TAKEN IN THE JOHN DAY RIVER

Trip No. 73   Wenaha Canyon
                                     Wallowa County
Alternates: *Umatilla County*
   Grande Ronde River
   Snake River

A most delightful backpacking or packhorse fishing trip in late spring or early summer is up the remote, spectacular, and beautiful canyon of the Wenaha River in Northeast Oregon. This thirty-five-mile-long river winds down through some of the most awesome wilderness in the west, along the Oregon-Washington boundary to the little trading village of Troy at the river's confluence with the Grande Ronde. You can reach Troy via State Highway 3 from Enterprise or Lewiston, Idaho, turning off at the Flora junction or at the Oasis Bridge over the Grande Ronde.

There are no roads up the Wenaha, but there is a good —and sometimes breathtaking—trail from Troy. There are several campgrounds in the lower section and some spike camps in the upper which are used by deer and elk hunters in season.

There is a winter steelhead and a spring chinook run up this river, too, but in the spring and summer the rainbow trout and dolly varden fishing is the thing to go for. That, and a soul-satisfying escape to a frontier as it once was.

Trip No. 74   Lower Grande Ronde
                                    Wallowa County
Alternates:
   Imnaha River
   Snake River

You can fish the Lower Grande Ronde most of the
year, except for the steelhead closure from April to June
and the salmon closure from June through August, and
you can float the lower river with guides and rubber rafts
for adventure. However, the inveterate winter steelhead-
er will find the ironhead fishing from late August through
the winter superb for not only drifting but also fly fishing. And what's more he'll have the river mostly to himself.

The entire lower river has some excellent pools and
drifts, but I would recommend starting with the pool at
the confluence with the Wenaha at Troy and working on
down.

You can reach Troy via State 3 from Enterprise or
Lewiston, Idaho, to the turn-off at Flora junction about
thirty-five miles north of Enterprise, or from the Oasis
Bridge across the Grande Ronde.

This is pretty hairy country in the winter months,
so go prepared. The temperature along the river, however, will be ten to fifteen degrees warmer than up in the
snow country.

Trip No. 75   Catherine Creek
                                Union County
Alternates:
   Grande Ronde River
   Thief Valley Reservoir

A beautiful all-around stream in the cattle and pine country of Eastern Oregon, Catherine Creek flows into the Grande Ronde River near Union and is about thirty miles long, It can be reached via State Highways 203 and 237 from La Grande or Baker.

This is not only an excellent steelhead and salmon stream, but is also one of the best trout waters in these parts, being well stocked with rainbows. It is heavily fished, however, and the trout are extremely wary. Salmon fishing is best in the late spring months; steelheading, in late winter and early spring. The trout rise best in summer and fall. Bait, lures, and flies all work.

Check the angling regulations carefully, for there are a number of exceptions and closures which apply.

Camping facilities are available at a state park right on the creek south of Union.

Catherine Creek is also a gateway to the Wallowa Mountains and is popular with deer and elk hunters.

Trip No. 76   Magone Lake
                             Grant County
Alternates:
  John Day River
  Middle Fork

Magone Lake is a Blue Mountains back country lake about eighty acres in size 4,900 feet up in Malheur National Forest. A popular spot, it contains excellent rainbow and brook trout, as well as some kokanees. Bait, lures, and flies all work, and some big trout are taken in the late summer and fall on conventional patterns.

A camping facility and boat launch sites contribute to Magone's popularity. Located north of John Day, it can be reached via U.S. 395 to the junction, thence by gravel road about fifteen miles east. Another road goes in from U.S. 26. Consult a local map.

This is also good deer country, and many hunters bring their fishing tackle.

CATHEDRAL ROCK, WITH THE JOHN DAY RIVER IN THE FOREGROUND

Trip No. 77   Upper Hells Canyon
                               Baker County
Alternates:
  Powder River
  Fish Lake

A series of low dams on the Snake River and their impoundments are known individually as Brownlee, Oxbow, and Hells Canyon but collectively as the Hells Canyon dams. The upstream pool is Brownlee, then comes Oxbow, and finally the newest and lowest, Hells Canyon Dam, which forms a twenty-two-mile-long lake in the historic mining district made famous by the old town of Homestead, Oregon, and the Kleinschmidt Grade on the Idaho side.

The fishing season is open all year 'round, although in midsummer the canyon of the Snake gets too hot for everyone but Californians. The best times are in spring and fall—and during the latter you can combine bird and deer hunting with the fishing.

These Snake impoundments have some of the best smallmouth bass, crappie, and catfish angling in the nation, although most of them are small. There is also planted rainbow trout, of course, and sturgeon fishing is fair to good. The dams have long since killed the famed anadromous fish runs in the upper Snake.

You can reach these impoundments from Baker on State 86 or from Huntington and Farewell Bend state park on a secondary road along the river.

Photo Courtesy Oregon State Highway Travel Division

THE GRAND CANYON OF THE SNAKE RIVER, FORMING THE
BOUNDARY BETWEEN OREGON AND IDAHO

Trip No. 78   Middle Snake
                                Wallowa County
Alternates:
  Grande Ronde River
  Imnaha River

With the possible exception of the upper Owyhee Canyon, the most inaccessible of all of Oregon's fishing spots is the "Middle Snake"—that portion of the Grand Canyon of the Snake from Lewiston, Idaho, to Battle Creek just below the new Hells Canyon Dam. At one point, below Hat Point on the rim of the canyon, the gorge is more than six thousand feet deep—the deepest one on the continent.

To get into this wild, rugged, and superbly beautiful wilderness (which, incidentally, the power combine now wants to flood with the proposed High Mountain Sheep Dam), you go by mail or private jet boat up from Lewiston ninety-three miles to the head of navigation. Or you hike or take a packhorse outfit in along the excellent Snake River Trail, which can be reached over several passes and saddles from the Oregon side. Sources of information are U.S. Forest Service, Portland; Joseph and Enterprise, Oregon, Lewiston, Idaho, chambers of commerce; Oregon Guides and Packers Association; and the Game Commission.

You can also reach the area via boat charter service or float trip from the new Hells Canyon Dam.

Spring and fall are best. Fishing includes bass, catfish, sturgeon, steelhead, and salmon.

Trip No. 79

Lostine River
Wallowa County

Alternates:
   Wallowa River
   High Lakes

The jump-off point for the Lostine River and its canyon which winds back up into the High Wallowas is the little cow town of Lostine on State 82 east of Elgin, near where it joins the Wallowa. There is a road of sorts up the river as far as the limits of the Eagle Cap Wilderness, and from there you can hike seven miles to the head of the river or to any of the several dozen jewel-like mountain lakes. The Lostine, in other words, is on the route to good alpine fishing.

The stream is heavily planted with trout and has some excellent fly, bait, and lure angling in the spring and fall. It is, however, closed to salmon and steelhead angling.

A good "hunter's fishing stream," the Lostine is in a beautiful setting, with several good campsites along its length.

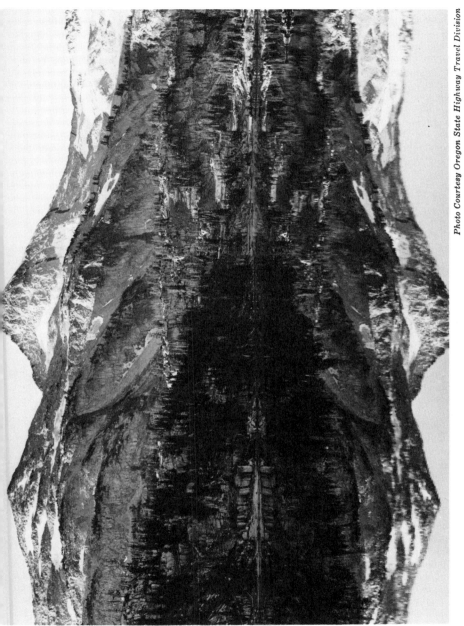

MOCCASIN LAKE REFLECTING EAGLE CAP MOUNTAIN

Photo Courtesy Oregon State Highway Travel Division

Trip No. 80   Minam River
                               Wallowa County
Alternates:
  None

With its head in the alp-like Eagle Cap Wilderness Area of the Wallowas, the Minam is truly a classic "wild river," and the Minam canyon is as intriguing as it sounds. A tributary of the Grande Ronde, it first flows into the Wallowa before plunging down into the Grande Ronde gorge at the highway bridge some fifteen miles east of Elgin on State 82. The stream is not accessible for its entire length, but there are a few miles of unimproved roads and trails along or close to much of it.

The steelhead angling is closed from April 1 to June 1, and the salmon from June 20 to September 1, although the regulations may vary from year to year. Check the *Synopsis*. The best steelhead and salmon fishing is in the winter months, with late fall and early spring next.

The stream also has excellent native and planted trout fishing, including some rare dolly varden, eastern brook, and rainbows. Fly fishing is good, although probably most anglers use bait or spinning gear. The river is not stocked, and the natives are wary.

Elgin and Wallowa are the nearest points for supplies and accommodations.

Trip No. 81   Upper John Day River
                               Grant County
Alternates:
   Magone Lake

One stretch of the fascinating geological "museum" of the John Day River gorge, between Prairie City and Twickenham, contains some surprisingly good trout fishing and some of the best steelheading in Oregon—although it is not generally known. *Caution:* Check the *Synopsis* of angling regulations for salmon and steelhead closures.

The John Day is not generally accessible by car, except for road crossings and the stretch along U.S. 26 and State 19. There is considerable private land along its watercourse, and permission is not readily available. It is semi-desert, alkaline and sagebrush country below Dayville, although the multi-colored, castellated, and truncated cones and outcroppings make it wildly beautiful. The river flows like an oasis through this region of fossil beds and rock formations dating back seventy-five million years. During the summer the river often dries up to a series of pools. Rattlesnakes are numerous along the moist green shoreline.

The "ghost" settlement of Twickenham is a fascinating remnant of early Oregon history, and there are also some good steelhead and trout holes nearby.

There are a number of good campsites along the canyon's course.

Photo Courtesy Oregon State Highway Travel Division

FLOWING NORTH THROUGH CENTRAL OREGON'S VAST COLUM-
BIA RIVER BASALT PLATEAU, THE JOHN DAY RIVER HAS EX-
POSED SOME OF THE WORLD'S MOST PRODUCTIVE FOSSIL BEDS

Trip No. 82   Middle Fork John Day
                               Grant County

Alternates:
   Magone Lake
   John Day River

There is a rough road along most of the length of the
Middle Fork, a major tributary of the John Day, which
flows out of the Blue Mountains and joins the main river
between Ritter and John Day. This is one of the best, and
least known, steelhead streams in this part of the state—
but be sure to check the *Synopsis* of regulations for exceptions. It also has some dark salmon occasionally, and
only the lower section is open to these anadromous fish.
Winter and early spring are the best times.

   The river is heavily stocked with rainbow trout and
the fly fishing, as well as bait and lure casting, is at times
terrific, particularly in spring and fall.

SMALLMOUTH BASS CAUGHT IN THE JOHN DAY RIVER

Trip No. 83   Lower Imnaha—Dug
                                      Bar
Alternates: *Wallowa County*
    Snake River
    Grande Ronde River

The Grand Canyon of the Imnaha is just as awesome as the Grand Canyon of the Snake (Hells Canyon) which is just over the ridge. In fact, these canyons run almost parallel to each other for thirty miles or so along the Oregon border, and this is the heart of the famous "Canyon Country" of Northeast Oregon.

The lower Imnaha, below the trading post of Imnaha, which is reached by good road from Joseph, is not as well known to anglers as the upper river. The entire river, of course, is a superb steelhead and salmon spawning stream and would be destroyed forever by the proposed High Mountain Sheep Dam on the Snake.

The lower Imnaha for about seven miles or so is entirely in private ownership and not easily accessible, although tantalizingly close. Then the canyon narrows and deepens as the river plunges toward the Snake. The road climbs up around the rimrock at dizzy heights and eventually brings you to Dug Bar on the Snake. It is a popular route for steelheaders and deer and chukar hunters who know the country. The Snake is open for fishing all year.

The Imnaha is a winter steelhead show, as well as a spring, summer, and fall trout stream with rainbow, dolly varden, and even a run of whitefish.

EASTERN OREGON CRAPPIE

Trip No. 84   Jubilee Lake
                               Union County
Alternates:
   Grande Ronde River
   Walla Walla River

A new lake which produced some fabulous trout fishing, Jubilee is located in the remote, high (4,800 feet), ponderosa pine back country of the Umatilla National Forest about thirteen miles northeast of Tollgate. It is best reached by State 204 from Elgin or Milton-Freewater.

About one-hundred acres in size, Jubilee was stocked in the late 1960s, and the Game Commission, with the cooperation of the Forest Service, intends to keep it that way. The fish run big and with proper management the lake will be one of the best in this part of the state.

It has picnic and trailer sites and will become increasingly popular over the years, as it is in a location convenient to Pendleton, Milton-Freewater, and Walla Walla, Washington. It is already a popular winter sports area and, of course, is a superb big game hunting region, bordering on the Wenaha Backcountry Area.

ANEROID LAKE IN THE WALLOWA MOUNTAINS

WALLOWA FALLS IN NORTHEASTERN OREGON

Trip No. 85   Upper Umatilla River
                               Umatilla County

Alternates:
  North Fork
  South Fork

Heading in the remote Blue Mountains, the upper section of the Umatilla River above Pendleton is heavily stocked by the Game Commission and the federal government on the portion that crosses the Indian Reservation. It is an excellent native trout stream, as well, noted for its good fly fishing, particularly in the Bingham Springs area. It is closed to salmon and steelhead above the Mission Bridge, however, and anglers should carefully check the *Synopsis* for exceptions and exclusions. On the Reservation lands, permission must be obtained from the tribal officials at Mission.

Access can be had from Pendleton via the Cayuse Road, and from State 11 and State 204 northeast of Pendleton at marked side roads.

Above Bingham Springs the South Fork is also an excellent but little-known fly fishing stream, accessible in the upper waters only by trail.

There are camping facilities in Umatilla National Forest.

Trip No. 86   South Fork Walla Walla
                               Umatilla County
Alternates:
  North Fork
  Umatilla River

The Walla Walla is closed to steelhead and salmon fishing above the confluence of the north and south forks (closed below from April 1 to November 30) but the river is heavily stocked with trout above the deadline and is open during the regular trout season.

Best time to fish it is in the spring, because in summer and fall the heavy use of the water for irrigation affects the stock.

A road follows the North Fork about half its distance, and access is difficult above that. There are also several unimproved roads in the watershed. There is considerable private property along the streams, although the river heads in national forest areas.

Milton-Freewater is the closest point for accommodations and service.

Trip No. 87   Wallowa River
                               Wallowa County
Alternates:
  Lostine River
  Grande Ronde River

A popular sparkling mountain stream flows out of the Wallowas, through well-known Wallowa Lake, then down through the "Land of Winding Waters" to its junction with the Lostine and Minam, thence into the Grande Ronde and the Snake. It is about eighty-three miles long and is open year 'round.

Late fall and spring are the best times for salmon from the Wallowa River. Steelhead is taken all winter long, with peaks in the late fall and early spring. Check the *Synopsis* for salmon and steelhead regulations.

The river is heavily stocked with trout and is usually an excellent and easily accessible stream for waders and fly casters. It contains rainbow, cutthroat, dolly varden, and eastern brook.

The fly fishing is best in the early fall.

The river can be reached via State 82 between Enterprise and Minam. There are a number of campsites and picnic areas.

ANTHONY LAKES,
SITUATED AT THE
FOOT OF GUNSIGHT
MOUNTAIN

BEAR LAKE IN THE
EAGLE CAP
WILDERNESS AREA

WALLOWA LAKE IN
NORTHEASTERN
OREGON

PART IX

SOUTHEAST OREGON

Canyon Cr. Mdws Res.

North

Silvies

Van

395

Malheur

Drewsey

Beulah
Reservoir

Westfall

Bully Cr. Res.

Willow Cr.

Vale

Ontario

201

201

Cairo

Nyssa

Parma

Harper

Malheur

River

20

Juntura

Malheur
River

Adrian

Harney

Warm
Springs
Res.

201

OWYHEE
DAM

Riverside

River

78

Lawen

Crane

Owyhee
Lake

M A L H E U R

Malheur
Lake

South

Princeton

Succor Cr.

Malloy
Ranch

Narrows

River

Shesville

206

Barton L.

E   Y

Happy
Valley

Cow
Lakes

Jordan Valley

Diamond

Krumbo Res.

Tenmile L.

78

Arock

Danner

Juniper
L.

Tudor L.

Owyhee

Antelope
Reservoir

Boca L.

Jordan

nchglen

Mann
L.

Rome

Fish L.
Blitzen

S T E E N S

M O U N T A I N

Blitzen R.

Burns Jct.

Owyhee

Roaring Springs
Ranch

Crooked Cr.
Spring

95

Three
Forks

Andrews

Alvord Lake

Whitehorse
Ranch

Basque Station

River

River

South Fork

Fields

Trout

Creek

Tum Tum L.

Little Owyhee

Denio

Trip No. 88   Owyhee Lake
                               Malheur County
Alternates:
  None

One of the most interesting fishing spots in the West is unique Owyhee Lake, a desert inland sea in the barren volcanic "moon country" of Southeast Oregon. The "lake" is actually a reservoir formed by a Bureau of Reclamation dam on the lower river. The impoundment is deep and backs up into the canyon for fifty miles or more, with only the lower five miles accessible by car.

Spring and fall are the best times; it's too hot in the summer. The best route in is from Ontario, Oregon, on the Idaho border via a good secondary road through some fascinating "rockhound" country to the dam site. There is some rainbow trout fishing below the dam. Above the dam a road is carved out of solid rock around the south shore for five miles to a state park and a privately owned moorage, motel, and resort.

The lake is full of bass, but they are hard to catch. The most popular fishing is for crappies, and this is fabulous. If you use plastic jig flies and don't catch a hundred a day, you just aren't fishing.

By boat you can explore hundreds of miles of primitive shoreline, and in the fall you can combine deer and chukar hunting in the upper sections with bass and crappie fishing. There is also an airstrip in the upper end and a Jeep road leading in to it.

Photo Courtesy Oregon State Highway Travel Division

OWYHEE LAKE, SOUTH OF ONTARIO, OREGON

*Photo Courtesy Oregon State
Highway Travel Division*

**THE OWYHEE
RIVER OF
EASTERN OREGON**

Trip No. 89   Strawberry Lake
                               Grant County
Alternates:
   Slide Lake
   Little Strawberry

A remote little pack-in lake of some fifty or sixty acres located in the Strawberry Mountain Wilderness of the Malheur National Forest has always appealed to me, not only because of its beautiful sugar pine wilderness setting, but also because of its name. Another Strawberry Lake, fifteen hundred miles eastward on the raw, barren prairies of North Dakota, was where I first went fishing with my dad.

This Strawberry, located in the Blue Mountain mining country of Oregon, southeast of Canyon City, can be reached via a secondary road from U.S. 26 at Prairie City. The road takes you within the wilderness area to the Strawberry Lake Camp. From there it is a mile hike to the big lake, with trails leading all over the wilderness.

Strawberry is open all year to fishing, but the spring and fall fly fishing is best. Rainbows go to eighteen inches. The angling for eastern brook is also good. The south end is best. No motors are allowed on the lake and no vehicles within the wilderness area.

This is not only an excellent, but fragile, fishing spot, but the wilderness itself is an inspiring paradise for the outdoors lover and deserving of a leisurely stay.

SCENIC BEAUTY IN
THE RUGGED
STRAWBERRY
MOUNTAIN AREA

STRAWBERRY LAKE

Trip No. 90   Malheur Reservoir
                               Malheur County

Alternates:
    Unity Reservoir
    Malheur River

For a dry country reservoir in the high desert of Eastern Oregon, the impoundment on the upper Malheur River is one of the best fishing spots in that part of the state. It is located northwest of Vale about fifteen miles off U.S. 26. Recently rehabilitated and restocked by the game commission, it is now a superb trout lake with limits common and some big ones going to four and five pounds.

It is not open all year like most reservoirs—only during the regular trout season. The fishing, even in the hottest part of the summer, has been excellent in recent years. The lake covers about twelve hundred acres, which is large for this part of the country. There are facilities for campers and picnickers.

Fly fishing in the early morning and evening is excellent during the late summer and fall.

Trip No. 91   Fish Lake
                               Harney County

Alternates:
   Delintment Lake
   Donner and Blitzen River

An oasis in the high sagebrush desert country of Eastern Oregon, Fish Lake is not only a well-stocked trout water with both legal rainbows and brooks, but its high carry-over from previous stockings makes it a top notch fly-fishing lake, although it is only about twenty acres in size.

The fly fishing is best in the fall, and many hunters coming to this part of the state bring along their rods to fill in the time in camp. Some of the trout will weigh two and three pounds.

You can reach Fish Lake from Frenchglen on the secondary road south along the Steens Mountain from Burns on state 205, about eighty miles.

There are camping and picnic facilities, trailer parking, boat rental and a resort at the lake.

Photo Courtesy Oregon State Highway Travel Division

KIGER GORGE IN THE STEENS MOUNTAIN COUNTRY

Trip No. 92   Emigrant Creek
                               Harney County
Alternates:
    Delintment Lake
    Malheur River

A tributary of the Silvies River which flows through Burns, Emigrant Creek got its name from the emigrant party that attempted the disastrous Meek Cut-off. It is now a top trout stream on the edge of the Ochoco National Forest and is heavily stocked with rainbows. Bait, lures, and flies all work here. Best time is spring and fall.

Campsites are available in the vicinity. Silvies, Burns, and Seneca are the nearest communities. From Burns the creek can be reached via gravel roads, and there are many such roads lending access along its thirty miles. Check on any highway map.

OWYHEE LAKE

Don Holm Photo

Trip No. 93   Donner und Blitzen
                                          River
Alternates: *Harney County*
    Krumbo Reservoir
    Fish Lake

I think my main reason for selecting Donner und Blitzen was its name, although it heads in the remote and beautiful Steens Mountain and meanders down into the Malheur Wildlife Refuge, and is regularly stocked by the federal agencies with cutthroat and rainbows. It is reached from Burns via State 205 to Frenchglen, although the best fishing is north of this picturesque little frontier post. Open down to Bridge Creek, the stream is accessible in a number of places by dirt and Jeep roads.

Watch for rattlesnakes at all times during the fishing season.

Trout as big as eighteen and twenty inches can be taken on bait, spinning lures, and flies. Local inquiry is recommended, as is checking the state angling *Synopsis*.

Campgrounds and camper parking are generally available in the area. Accommodations and services are available at Burns, with some also at Frenchglen.

Bring cameras for some wildlife photography.

Trip No. 94   Mann Lake
                               Harney County
Alternates:
   Fifteencent Lake
   Juniper Lake

A fragile high desert lake "a hundred miles from no-where," as one old cowboy in Burns told me, Mann Lake is about 245 acres in size in "normal" years, and in those years it really puts out some astonishing cutthroat trout fishing. It is regularly stocked and has a carry-over of native cuts up to sixteen inches. During drought years it is subject to extreme draw-down when the bulk of the fish population is lost. However, when normal water levels return it is heavily stocked again.

Located on the east slope of Steens Mountain, Mann Lake is best reached from Burns south via State 78 to Follyfarm, then right on gravel road for twenty-five miles past Fifteencent, Tudor, and Juniper lakes.

There are no supplies available in this region, and very little help if you get lost or broken down. It is, however, a fascinating region for the photographer, rockhound, and chukar and deer hunter.

Fishing in "normal" years is best in the spring and possibly late fall.

Trip No. 95   Cow Lakes
                               Malheur County
Alternates:
   Owyhee Lake
   Snake River

Located just west of U.S. 95, the small lava-desert
Cow Lakes can be reached from Jordan Valley, the
Basque village near the Oregon-Idaho line, on a gravel
road along Cow Creek. The upper lake was treated and
restocked in the early 1960s and if lucky you'll find some
truly superb trout fishing when you get there. The Game
Commission management of this fishery is expected to
continue, so it should remain an outstanding spot for this
part of the country.

The big lake, which is about 950 acres in size, is the
one to fish at present. Bait, lures, and flies should work
all through the season. Best way to fish this lake, as on
most small bodies of water in this region, is by small boat,
drifting or using oars.

The little-known Lava Beds of Southeast Oregon are
located just south and west of the Cow Lakes.

BLACK CRAPPIE FROM OWYHEE LAKE

OWYHEE RIVER CANYON

THE OREGON COAST
Northern half

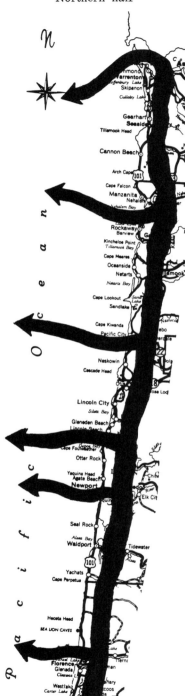

THE OREGON COAST
Southern half

PART X

OFFSHORE OREGON

Trip No. 96   Cape Kiwanda
                               Tillamook County
Alternates:
   Nestucca River
   Trask River
   Tillamook Bay

Launching a famed Kiwanda dory through the surf in the lee of the Cape is, says Oregon State Representative Paul Hanneman, who is a fishing guide between legislative sessions, a couple moments of stark terror followed by a half day or so on the beautiful Pacific Ocean just outside the surf line. These dories, evolved during the past hundred years, are light and seaworthy craft and a local institution. The dorymen usually charge about $10-$15 a person and carry three or four sportsmen in each. After shoving off from the beach, the doryman starts the outboard motor and quickly claws off from the breakers.

The fishing is done mostly from a point beginning at the tip of Cape Kiwanda south to the mouth of the Nestucca, inside Haystack Rock. From May until September it's a superb salmon fishery; and the rest of the year, when the ocean is flat enough for the dorymen to get out, it is a superb bottom fishing spot for halibut, flounder, ling cod, rockfish, and many other unexploited but excellent marine species.

At any time, the Kiwanda dory fishing is without doubt the most unusual experience along the West Coast tidal waters.

OFFSHORE SALMON

Don Holm Photo

FIGHTING AN ALBACORE TUNA FAR OFFSHORE IN THE
"BLUE WATER" FORTY MILES OUT

Don Holm Photo

Trip No. 97   Blue Water Tuna

The Northwest's most adventurous fishing trip is unknown to most anglers but will someday be the region's most important saltwater sport fishery. This is the run for the blue water off the continental shelf, out where the pelagic schools of albacore are found.

The albacore is one of the World's fastest, toughest, and most prized game fish—and good eating, too. Until recently it was not generally known that these schools of tuna, well-known in warmer waters, pass close to northwest coasts on their circular migrations around the Pacific Ocean. They are always found in the blue water, which has a surface temperature between 60 and 68 degrees. Along the Northwest coast blue water occurs anywhere from ten to two hundred miles out, depending on the current and wind. The tuna are present from May to October at least, with August and September the best months. In these waters they average fifteen to thirty pounds in size.

A new charter fleet, geared especially for overnight trips, is slowly building in the Northwest. At this writing, Ilwaco and Westport in Washington, and Warrenton, Depoe Bay, Newport, and Coos Bay in Oregon are the principal ports. At present the fishing is all done by trolling feather jigs, but inevitably live bait will come into use here, as it has in California. You'll need heavy sport gear with forty- to fifty-pound-test line.

Don Holm Photo

ALBACORE IN THE NET

Trip No. 98   Columbia Bar
                               Clatsop County
Alternates:
  Westport, Wash.
  Tillamook Bay

When I first fished for salmon at the mouth of the Columbia River, most sport angling was done inside the river trolling plugs and spoons and only lasted a few weeks in August. Local experts had decreed that this was how it was to be. Then, in the 1950s, some adventurous salmon moochers from Puget Sound came down, bringing fresh herring, and revolutionized the "industry," as they say. Today you'd have a time trying to find a plug or spoon used. Also practically all the salmon fishing is now done *outside*, on the ocean, not just in August, but all summer long from about the end of May to the end of September.

The area off the Columbia is the greatest salmon fishing spot in the world. On a typical day in August you'll find anywhere from 1,000 to 2,000 boats there, each carrying from six to twenty people. And the average catch all summer long is one salmon per rod per day.

Unless you have your own sea-goin' boat, figure on getting aboard a charter boat out of Warrenton or Hammond on the Oregon side, or Ilwaco on the Washington side.

You need heavy salmon or steelhead gear, one to two ounces of lead and herring hook-ups. You can, if you like, rent an outfit from the skipper. Everything else is furnished.

You haven't lived until you've fished for salmon off the "Bar."

OFFSHORE SALMON FISHING   *Don Holm Photo*

Don Holm Photo

SALMON CATCH OFF THE COLUMBIA RIVER

Trip No. 99   Depoe Bay
                               Lincoln County
Alternates:
    Siletz Bay
    Siletz River

Oregon's most picturesque "dog hole," Depoe Bay, is a sailor's port in a storm in a long stretch of wild coast-line. Experienced skippers tell me that this port, hairy as it looks from any angle, with its narrow entrance, is still one of the safest to enter during bad weather.

Located at the town of Depoe Bay on U.S. 101, just north of Newport, this natural harbor has been greatly improved. It has a Coast Guard station, small boat moorage and docks, and a charter fleet which operates all year around—for bottom fishing in winter and salmon fishing in spring, summer, and fall, with a little blue water tuna fishing in August and September. There is no fishing in the bay itself.

All facilities are located here, including some luxury resort motels, fish canneries, and boat works. It is also a popular tourist spot and, in winter when the storms rage, a prime attraction for sightseers.

Don Holm Photo

LANDING AN ALBACORE TUNA

Trip No. 100   Winchester Bay
Douglas County

Alternates:
   Umpqua River
   Smith River

Located at and below Reedsport on U.S. 101 north of Coos Bay, Winchester Bay is a major sport and commercial salmon fishing port, with a superb small boat basin called "Salmon Harbor." During the salmon season in spring, summer, and fall, the basin is jammed with boats, private and charter; and the many excellent trailer parks, campgrounds, and motels around the harbor are filled. A carnival atmosphere prevails and it's easy to see that this is a major West Coast sport center.

The bar at Winchester Bay, however, is probably the most dangerous on the coast, which accounts for a full-scale Coast Guard rescue station on the site. Most boats get into trouble because they ignore warnings, but if caution and common sense are used, offshore anglers have no problem.

The offshore fishery, which at times is fantastic, gets started in May or June and runs through until September, weather being the deciding factor at all times. The salmon mostly are coho, with some chinook early in the season. Striped bass, ocean perch, flounder, halibut, clams, crabs, and bottom fish also enhance the bay and beach fishing.

Trip No. 101   Stonewall Bank
                                Off Newport
Alternates:
   Yaquina Bay
   Depoe Bay
   Alsea Bay

At this writing, anglers fish for marine game species only incidentally to salmon, but they are rapidly becoming aware of the vast, almost untouched, sport fishery categorized "Offshore." Currently the total annual take is between two and five million pounds, but this will increase sharply in the next few years.

This is an all year 'round fishery, although during inclement weather and in the winter most of it is done from jetties, rocks, and beaches. But when you can get "outside" the fishing is almost always excellent on the offshore banks such as Stonewall Bank off Newport, the Cod Hole off Cape Kiwanda, the Rogue Reefs off Gold Beach and similar places along the coast that were formerly worked only by commercial trawlers.

The most common species are ling cod, halibut, flounder, sea perch, kelp greenling, cabezon, and numerous species of the big rockfish family, some of which are often called locally "sea bass."

Fishing for the offshore—or perhaps more accurately, "alongshore"—bottom species, you can use salmon or steelhead gear, but the free-spooling conventional reel is preferred to spinning reels. Bait includes kelp worms, clam necks, herring chunks, and jigs—all of which are obtainable at local harbors.

ROCKFISH CAUGHT AT
COOS BAY

Don Holm Photo

Don Holm Photo

THE AUTHOR AND A
CATCH OF "TOOTHY
CRITTERS" OFF THE
OREGON COAST

Don Holm Photo
TUNA FISHING OFF THE COAST OF OREGON IN A
KIWANDA DORY